GLOBETROTTER™
Travel Guide

NAMIBIA

WILLIE AND SANDRA OLIVIER

NEW
HOLLAND

NEW
HOLLAND

★★★ Highly recommended
★★ Recommended
★ See if you can

Fifth edition published in 2006
by New Holland Publishers (UK) Ltd
London • Cape Town • Sydney • Auckland
First published in 1994
10 9 8 7 6 5 4 3 2 1

website: www.newhollandpublishers.com

Garfield House, 86 Edgware Road
London W2 2EA, United Kingdom

80 McKenzie Street
Cape Town 8001, South Africa

14 Aquatic Drive, Frenchs Forest
NSW 2086, Australia

218 Lake Road, Northcote
Auckland, New Zealand

Distributed in the USA by
The Globe Pequot Press, Connecticut

ISBN 1 84537 575 0

Publishing Manager: Thea Grobbelaar
DTP Cartographic Manager: Genené Hart
Editors: Nicky Steenkamp, Sandie Vahl,
Thea Grobbelaar
Design and DTP: Nicole Bannister, Mandy Moss
Cartography: Tanja Spinola, Genené Hart,
Nicole Bannister
Reproduction by Hirt & Carter (Pty) Ltd, Cape Town
Printed and bound by Times Offset (M) Sdn. Bhd.,
Malaysia

Photographic credits:
Anthony Bannister, page 25 [ABPL]; Joe Brooks,
page 83 [PHOTO ACCESS]; Gerald Cubitt, pages
8, 14, 16, 21, 26, 27, 28, 40, 41, 44, 53, 57, 58,
64, 66, 69, 95, 97, 100, 104, 105, 108; Buster
Culverwell, page 68 [African Images]; Roger de la
Harpe, pages 19, 33, 51 [ABPL], 54, 55, 72, 84;
Charles Didcott, page 52; Gerhardus du Plessis,
page 80 [PHOTO ACCESS]; Jean du Plessis, pages
4, 7, 9, 11, 18, 20, 23, 34, 35, 48, 63, 67 left, 73,
76, 79, 81, 82, 85, 87, 88, 89, 96, 111, 112;
Kerstin Geier, page 24 [ABPL]; Clem Haagner,
pages 38 [ABPL], 119 [ABPL]; Corrie Hansen,
page 56; Leonard Hoffmann, title page [IOA];
Johan Jooste, page 37; Walter Knirr, cover [IOA];
Namibian Ministry of Information, page 17;
National Archives of Namibia, page 13; Robert
Nunnington, page 10 [ABPL]; Willie and Sandra
Olivier, pages 36, 39, 47, 50, 98, 113, 116; Peter
Pickford, pages 67 right [IOA], 102 [IOA];
Brendan Ryan, page 65; Karl Switak, page 71
[ABPL]; Mark van Aardt, pages 32, 103, 117; Hein
von Hörsten, pages 99 [ABPL], 115; Friedrich von
Hörsten, pages 92, 101; Patrick Wagner, pages 6
[PHOTO ACCESS], 49 [PHOTO ACCESS], 60
[PHOTO ACCESS], 70 [PHOTO ACCESS], 90
[PHOTO ACCESS], 118 [PHOTO ACCESS].
[ABPL: ABPL Photo Library; IOA: Images of Africa]

Although every effort has been made to ensure that
this guide is up to date and current at time of going
to print, the Publisher accepts no responsibility or
liability for any loss, injury or inconvenience
incurred by readers or travellers using this guide.

Keep us Current
Information in travel guides is apt to change, which
is why we regularly update our guides. We'd be
grateful to receive feedback if you've noted some-
thing we should include in our updates. If you have
new information; please share it with us by writing
to the Publishing Manager, Globetrotter, at the
office nearest to you (addresses on this page). The
most significant contribution to each new edition
will receive a free copy of the updated guide.

Cover: *Dramatic scenery – sand dunes reflected
in the water.*
Title page: *Quiver trees, southern Namibia.*

CONTENTS

1. **Introducing Namibia** 5
   The Land 6
   History in Brief 12
   Government and Economy 19
   The People 23

2. **Windhoek and Surrounds** 29
   Windhoek 30
   Mariental and Surrounds 37
   Herero and Mbanderu Processions 40

3. **Southern Namibia** 45
   The Southern Hinterland 46
   The Fish River Canyon and Ai-Ais 50
   The Diamond Coast 52

4. **The Namib** 61
   The Coast 62
   The Namib-Naukluft Park 66

5. **Skeleton Coast and Kaokoveld** 77
   National West Coast Recreation Area 78
   Damaraland 80
   Skeleton Coast Park 87
   Kaokoland 89

6. **Etosha and the North** 93
   The Erongos 94
   The Waterberg Plateau Park 96
   Etosha National Park 99
   Private Game Reserves 103
   The North 105

7. **Kavango and Caprivi** 109
   Bushmanland 110
   Kavango 111
   West Caprivi 115
   East Caprivi 116

Travel Tips 122

Index 127

1
Introducing Namibia

Covering 824,269km² (318,250 sq miles), Namibia is a country of contrasting landscapes ranging from the world's oldest desert to rugged mountains, dense woodlands and lily-carpeted waterways. As a result, its fascinating plant and animal life is equally varied.

Windhoek, the capital, is situated among the rolling hills of the central highlands. Here, modern office blocks contrast with German colonial buildings and their pitched roofs. In the south, **Ai-Ais**, with its thermal springs, is tucked away among rugged mountainous terrain along the Fish River, while on the coast tranquil **Lüderitz** offers a retreat from the heat of the interior.

Namibia's premier holiday town **Swakopmund** is a pleasant coastal resort that can be used as a base for day excursions to the seal colony at **Cape Cross**, the **Namib Desert** with its stark gravel plains and **Sandwich Harbour**. The dune sea surrounding **Sossusvlei**, south of the Kuiseb River, can only be explored from **Sesriem**, on the edge of the desert; the rugged **Naukluft Mountains** are a hikers' paradise.

A four-wheel-drive is required for an expedition to the arid, extremely rugged **Kaokoland** in the northwest, but several tourist attractions in **Damaraland** and the southern part of the **Skeleton Coast National Park** are easily accessible by car.

At **Etosha National Park** with its shimmering pan, the large number of game is the attraction. **Mahango** and **Khaudum** game parks to the east also offer excellent game-viewing in a more wilderness atmosphere.

TOP ATTRACTIONS

*** Etosha National Park: a sanctuary to thousands of typical plains animals and surrounding a large saltpan.
*** Namib-Naukluft Park: a fascinating desert of endless gravel plains, a vast dune sea and rugged mountains.
** Fish River Canyon: the second largest in the world, up to 549m (1801ft) deep.
** Swakopmund: a coastal resort with beautifully pre-served colonial buildings.
** Waterberg Plateau Park: a geological formation with rare mammal species and a variety of hiking trails.

Opposite: *A gigantic sand dune at Sossusvlei.*

HIGHEST MOUNTAINS

Namibia's highest mountain, the **Brandberg**, does not form part of the escarpment chain, but rises abruptly from the surrounding gravel plains. Its peak, **Königstein**, with an altitude of 2579m (8461ft), was first ascended in 1918 by a party of three. The second highest peak in the country is the **Molkte-Blick** at 2483m (8146ft) in the Auas Mountains just south of Windhoek; third highest is the table-top 2351m (7713ft) **Gamsberg** on the edge of the Khomas Hochland.

Opposite: *A palm-fringed segment of the mighty Kunene River.*
Below: *Travellers in four-wheel-drive vehicles cross the desolate, hauntingly beautiful Marienfluss valley in Kaokoland.*

THE LAND
Plateau, Mountains and Plains
The topography of Namibia is characterized by a narrow coastal plain and a vast inland plateau that are separated by a rugged escarpment.

The **coastal plain** extends eastwards from the coast for between 80km (50 miles) and 120km (74.5 miles) to the escarpment. With an average annual rainfall of between about 10mm (0.4in) a year at the coast and 150mm (6in) in the Pro-Namib along the eastern edge of the desert, this region is an extremely arid tract of land.

The **escarpment** forms part of the Great Escarpment of southern Africa that extends from southern Angola in an arc to the Ukhahlamba Drakensberg and Mpumalanga Drakensberg. In Namibia it is characterized by a deeply eroded mountain chain stretching discontinuously from the Kunene River in the north to the Orange River in the south. The central highlands, a landscape of dissected rolling hills, are known as the **Khomas Hochland**.

East of the escarpment lies the **inland plateau**, an area of vast plains fringed by low mountains, scattered hills and *inselbergen* (island mountains). Further east, the landscape is dominated by low, rolling **Kalahari dunes**.

The **Caprivi**, in the far northeast of the country, is a region of rivers, narrow water channels and woodlands and is unlike any other part of Namibia.

Rivers
Although the landscape is crisscrossed by a number of rivers, they are often dry for several years as a result of the erratic rainfall. However, after heavy rains these **dry river courses** are turned into torrents, racing down to the sea where they discharge their muddy

load. The underground water supply is recharged by these floods, providing a vital source of moisture for trees and animals during dry periods.

The only perennial rivers in Namibia are shared with its neighbours. In the south, the **Orange River** forms the border with South Africa for about 500km (311 miles), while the mighty **Kunene River** in the north forms part of Namibia's border with Angola for about 325km (202 miles). Winding through a primaeval landscape, the Kunene is characterized by thundering waterfalls, raging white-water rapids and tranquil streams. Further east, the **Kavango River** gushes over a series of cascades, the best known of which is the

Popa Falls, before continuing its journey to the famed Okavango Delta in Botswana.

Still further east, the **Kwando River** forms the boundary between Namibia, Angola and Zambia in the north, and after making its way through the Caprivi Strip, it serves as the border between Namibia and Botswana. Here it breaks up into a labyrinth of channels, islands and oxbow lakes to form the vast Linyanti Swamps. In the far northeast the **Zambezi River** serves as the frontier between Namibia and Zambia before plunging over the Victoria Falls in Zimbabwe.

Seas and Shores

Namibia's coastline of 1400km (2253 miles) is remarkably even and there are only three major bays – Lüderitz, Sandwich and Walvis Bay. The coast is washed by the cold **Benguela Current**, which is partly responsible for the extremely arid conditions here and causes dense fog

---

RICHES FROM THE SEA

Despite the adverse climatic conditions created by the cold Atlantic Ocean, conditions are ideal for marine life, and the offshore waters of Namibia are among the richest fishing grounds in the world. **Demersal fishing** is the most important component of the fishing industry and concentrates on hake and monkfish. The bulk of pelagic catches (pilchards and juvenile horse mackerel) is processed into fish meal and oil, and pilchards are also canned. Kingklip, sole and tuna are other valuable marine resources.

and low clouds for up to 120 days a year. As a result, the coastal region is uninhabited, except for Oranjemund and Lüderitz in the south, and Walvis Bay, Swakopmund and Henties Bay further north. Moderate temperatures on the coast attract many holiday-makers escaping from the excessive midsummer heat in the interior.

Increasing attention is being paid to offshore diamond mining along Namibia's southern coast, while promising gas reserves have been discovered 150km (93 miles) off the coast of Oranjemund.

FACTS AND FIGURES

Highest point: Königstein (2579m; 8461ft).
Highest waterfall: Ruacana at 120m (394ft) high.
Highest sand dune: at Sossusvlei (325m; 1069ft).
Biggest dam: Hardap (25km²; 10 sq miles).
Largest meteorite: Hoba Meteorite (about 60 tonnes).
Deepest canyon: Fish River Canyon, (549m; 1801ft).

Climate

With an unpredictable annual **rainfall**, averaging 270mm (10.5in), and a very high evaporation rate, Namibia is largely an arid country, and the Namib Desert is one of the driest areas in the world. Except in the southwestern corner of the country, a winter-rainfall area, more than half of the precipitation is recorded between October and March, and usually occurs as violent **thunderstorms** during mid-afternoon or early evening.

Daytime **temperatures** in summer are usually high, peaking at over 40°C (104°F) in the extreme south and north of the country. The central highlands are usually a bit cooler. Winter days are mild and minimum temperatures are low.

COMPARATIVE CLIMATE CHART	WINDHOEK				ETOSHA				SWAKOPMUND			
	SUM	AUT	WIN	SPR	SUM	AUT	WIN	SPR	SUM	AUT	WIN	SPR
	JAN	APR	JULY	OCT	JAN	APR	JULY	OCT	JAN	APR	JULY	OCT
MAX TEMP. °C	36	29	25	35	33	31	26	35	21	20	18	6
MIN TEMP. °C	11	4	5	12	16	15	6	17	15	13	9	11
MAX TEMP. °F	96	84	78	95	92	87	78	94	69	67	64	62
MIN TEMP. °F	51	39	41	53	60	58	42	62	59	55	47	51
HOURS OF SUN	9	9	9	10	8	9	10	9	7	7	8	7
RAINFALL in	3	1.5	0	0.5	3	1	0	0	0	0	0	0
RAINFALL mm	78	38	1	11	75	26	0	7	1	1	0	0

Plant Life

As a result of the dramatic changes in climatic conditions from the coast to the northeast of the country, Namibia has a rich variety of plant life, ranging from hardy desert plants that can survive for years without rain to papyrus reeds and tropical trees.

The fascination of Namibia's flora, however, does not lie in its diversity, but in the number of species that have adapted to survive in the inhospitable Namib Desert and the Pro-Namib. Best known is the **Welwitschia mirabilis**, a unique species that has commanded the attention of botanists worldwide since it was first recorded in 1859 (see page 68).

Some desert-adapted plants take in water through their leaves, while others have an extensive, shallow root system that enables them to absorb condensed fog.

A region of particular botanical interest is the winter-rainfall area of southwestern Namibia. The sandy gravel plains and rocky mountain slopes of this arid region are the habitat of a large number of the country's protected plants. Among these are the interesting **elephant's trunk**, which at a distance resembles a person, and a fascinating variety of **stone plants** (*Lithops*). Further inland towards the south the much-photographed **quiver tree**, or *kokerboom*, is found.

Nearly 60% of the land's vegetation is characterized by **savannas**, ranging from dwarf shrub in the south to camelthorn in the east and mopane in the northwest.

The dense **woodlands** in the northeast are in sharp contrast to the sparsely vegetated Namib Desert, while the **wetlands** of Eastern Caprivi are a complete surprise to the first-time visitor.

Opposite: *Sand dunes meet the Atlantic Ocean along the barren coast of the central Namib Dessert.*
Below: *The drought-resistant quiver tree.*

Above: *This desert-adapted gemsbok and its calf feed on moisture-laden plants to survive the dry periods.*

GEMSBOK

The gemsbok, relative of the Arabian oryx, is widely distributed throughout Namibia. It is an elegant antelope with magnificent straight horns and distinctive black and white facial marks. The horns of both sexes can reach a length of up to 1.2m (4ft). Well adapted to live in arid areas, the gemsbok can go for long periods without drinking water, and a complex network of blood vessels beneath the brain enables it to survive body temperatures of more than 45°C (113°F). This distinctive antelope features both on Namibia's coat of arms and on the 100 dollar banknote.

Wildlife

Namibia's wildlife ranges from highly specialized reptiles and beetles that are endemic to the Namib Desert to semi-aquatic and aquatic species that are restricted to the wetlands in north-eastern Namibia.

From the accounts of early travellers it is clear that Namibia was a wildlife paradise just over a century ago. Giraffe and even rhino lived on the outer fringes of the desert, while large herds of antelope ventured deep into the Namib in search of grazing after good rains. Hunting, poaching and, above all, the restriction of migratory animals' movement by fences have reduced game numbers in many of the commercial farming regions. Game populations in communal conservancies in the northwest and northeast of the country have shown encouraging increases.

Fortunately, though, land has been set aside as game reserves, the best known being the **Etosha National Park**. It is a sanctuary for large herds of typical plains animals such as springbok, blue wildebeest and elephant, and it has the largest black rhino population in Africa.

In the northeast of the country **Khaudum Game Park**, a truly wild tract of land, is an important refuge for the endangered roan. Several antelope species such as red lechwe, waterbuck, reedbuck and sitatunga are restricted to the wetlands in the far northeast of Namibia where the prime attraction is the prolific birdlife.

Far too often the fascinating variety of lesser creatures are overlooked. Despite its hostile environment, the dunes and gravel plains of the **Namib-Naukluft Park** are the home to many endemic reptiles and beetles.

Conserving Namibia's Natural Heritage

Nearly 15% of the land enjoys conservation status. This is not only well above the percentage recommended by the IUCN, but also one of the highest in Africa.

Prior to independence, game parks were set aside without considering the people living in the area or any benefits to surrounding communities. However, Namibia's conservation authorities have since adopted a policy of **community-based natural resource management**. Communal conservancies have been established throughout the country, but mainly in the northwest and northeast. Control over the wildlife resources in these areas not only provides an incentive to the inhabitants to conserve the wildlife, but communities also benefit directly from natural resources and tourism.

Commercial farmers have also played an important role in conservation. In 1967 ownership of ordinary game on their property was transferred from the State to landowners. This provided an incentive to farmers to protect wildlife on their land and laid the foundation of Namibia's lucrative game-farming industry. There are numerous hunting farms throughout the country.

Non-governmental organizations (NGOs) helped to prevent the desert-dwelling animals of Damaraland and Kaokoland from being wiped out completely. NGOs still active in this field include Save the Rhino Trust and the South African-based Endangered Wildlife Trust. The South African Nature Foundation (now WWF South Africa) gave much-needed financial support and publicity during the initial anti-poaching campaign.

CONSERVATION AND THE CONSTITUTION

The Namibian Constitution guarantees the protection of the environment. **Article 95 (f)** provides for the promotion and maintenance of the welfare of the people by the State by adopting policies aimed at preserving the environment. **Article 95 (c)**, establishes an Ombudsman to investigate, amongst others, complaints related to the environment.

Below: *Well-nourished zebra in Etosha. The park is home to thousands of these strikingly marked animals.*

HISTORY IN BRIEF

There is evidence that people lived in Namibia for several thousand years during the **Stone Age**. What is probably the oldest rock paintings discovered on the African continent were unearthed in a cave in the Hunsberg, north of the Orange River, between 1969 and 1982. The paintings were executed on flat rocks during the Middle Stone Age, and have been dated at between 27,000 and 25,000 years old.

Towards the end of the Stone Age **San hunter–gatherers**, also referred to as Bushmen, lived in scattered groups throughout the country. They were divided into three main groups, and although their hunting and gathering way of life imposed certain similarities, they were culturally distinct and spoke different languages.

The earliest record of the pastoral **Khoikhoi** who migrated to Namibia dates back about 2600 years. Initially they had only fat-tailed sheep with long legs, but acquired cattle later. They moved about constantly in search of grazing, and the remains of their settlements can be seen throughout Namibia, even along the Namib coast.

Bantu-speaking people also migrated into Namibia and settled in the north of the country, while the **Herero**, a nation of pastoralists, settled in central and eastern Namibia. Other groups, such as the **Oorlam Nama**, crossed the Orange River in the early 1800s, and the **Basters** came to Namibia from the Northern Cape in the late 1860s.

The first **European** to set foot along the Namib coast was the Portuguese explorer, Diego Cão, who landed at Cape Cross in 1486. Although whalers and other vessels used Walvis Bay and Sandwich Bay as harbours for more than two centuries, it was not until March 1878 that Britain annexed Walvis Bay and the area surrounding it.

Germany also began extending its influence in Africa, and on 24 April 1884 an

---

HISTORICAL CALENDAR

January 1486: Portuguese explorer Diego Cão erects *padrão* at Cape Cross.
12 March 1878: Britain annexes Walvis Bay enclave.
24 April 1884: German Protectorate declared over Lüderitz and surrounding area.
11 January 1904: Herero Uprising against German colonial rule. Subsequent extermination of Herero people ordered by Von Trotha.
9 July 1915: German troops surrender to armed forces of Union of South Africa during First World War.

17 December 1920: League of Nations entrusts South West Africa to Union of South Africa as a Mandate.
10 December 1959: Under apartheid rule resistance to forced removals in Windhoek results in 13 people being killed by South African Police.
26 August 1966: First clash between SWAPO soldiers and South African forces.
27 October 1966: United Nations General Assembly adopts Resolution 2145, terminating South Africa's Mandate over South West Africa.

21 July 1971: International Court of Justice rules SA's presence in Namibia illegal.
4 May 1978: SWAPO members killed in a South African attack on Cassinga in Angola.
29 September 1978: United Nations Security Council adopts Resolution 435 outlining a solution to the conflict.
17 June 1985: Five-party Transitional Government of National Unity inaugurated.
1 April 1989: United Nations Resolution 435 implemented.
21 March 1990: Namibia gains Independence.

area surrounding Lüderitz was declared a protectorate. Several other protectorates were also declared, and 'protection treaties' were signed with some of the tribes. By the end of 1884 German rule was firmly established.

However, the charismatic Chief of the Witbooi Nama, **Hendrik Witbooi**, refused to sign a 'protection treaty' and on 12 April 1893 the German *Schutztruppe* attacked his stronghold at Hoornkrans. Witbooi then adopted guerrilla warfare tactics and it was not until August 1894 that at last a treaty was signed between the Germans and the Witbooi after a nine-day battle in the Naukluft Mountains.

Namibians were systematically dispossessed of their land by the German colonial administration and, fearing the loss of more land, the Herero under **Maherero** rose against German rule on 11 January 1904. The uprising started while the Germans were engaged in quelling an uprising by the **Bondelswart Nama** in the south. The Herero were finally defeated at the Battle of the Waterberg on 11 August 1904 and forced to flee into the waterless wastes in the east of the territory, while others went into exile in Botswana, then called Bechuanaland. Tens of thousands of Herero died in the war and of hunger and thirst and the genocide that followed; about 9000 men, women and children were taken prisoner.

Other indigenous people also took up arms against the Germans. In the north, several hundred **Ndonga** warriors attacked Fort Namutoni on 28 January 1904, while in the south of the country **Hendrik Witbooi** declared war against the Germans on 3 October 1904, a struggle that was to last until the end of 1906.

Following the declaration of the **First World War** on 4 August 1914, the South African Union forces invaded the country, and on 9 July 1915 the German troops surrendered at Kilometre 500 near Otavi.

On 17 December 1920 the League of Nations confirmed South Africa's **Mandate** over South West Africa.

Above: *Jan Jonker Afrikaner, son of Jonker Afrikaner (see page 40), became chief of the Oorlam Nama in 1863.*

VON TROTHA'S EXTERMINATION ORDER

After the defeat of the **Herero** in August 1904, General Lothar Von Trotha, issued his notorious extermination order: 'The Herero nation must now leave the country … Within the German frontier every Herero, with or without a rifle, with or without cattle, will be shot.'

THE ODENDAAL PLAN

In keeping with South Africa's policy of **separate development**, a commission was appointed in 1962 under the chairmanship of F. H. Odendaal to devise a **homeland system** for Namibia. Eleven 'bantustans' for the indigenous people, covering 332,567km^2 (128,404 sq miles), or 40% of the country's surface, were proposed, and legislative assemblies were introduced for whites and coloureds. In 1968 representative authorities were established for the different population groups, but the International Court of Justice ruling of June 1971 made it clear that South Africa could not declare the 'bantustans' independent. Ethnic administrations were maintained in these 'homelands' until just before the implementation of Resolution 435.

Hardly any new administrative structures were adopted by the new rulers, and white settlement was expanded.

In the north, **Chief Mandume ya Ndemufayo** resisted territorial demands, while the **Bondelswart** took up arms in the south when the South African government interfered in the succession of their chiefs.

After the **Second World War**, the League of Nations was replaced by the United Nations (UN). South Africa's request to the UN to incorporate South West Africa as a fifth province was turned down; in turn South Africa refused to place the territory under UN guardianship. This heralded the start of a lengthy dispute.

The victory of the National Party in the 1948 election in South Africa meant the introduction of **apartheid** in both South Africa and the occupied territory.

The **South West Africa National Union (SWANU)** was founded in August 1959 as a protest to the continued illegal occupation of Namibia. The following month, SWANU was joined by the **Owamboland People's Organization (OPO)**, which was initially founded in Cape Town in 1958 as the Owamboland People's Congress to campaign for the abolition of the contract labour system. Enforced separate residential areas for different race groups was just one aspect of

the policy of apartheid. Resistance to the **forced removal** of people from the Old Location in Windhoek to the Katutura township in December 1959 was ruthlessly crushed by the South African Police. Eleven people were killed and more than 60 wounded in what has become known as Namibia's Sharpeville Massacre.

The alliance between SWANU and the OPO was shortlived, and on 19 April 1960 the OPO was transformed into a broad-based national movement, the **South West Africa People's Organization (SWAPO)**, with the aim of liberating the Namibian people from colonial oppression and exploitation. By now it had become apparent that liberation would not be achieved through UN intervention alone. In 1961 SWAPO decided to prepare for an **armed struggle**, and on 18 July 1966 issued a statement saying that it had no alternative but to take to arms to bring an end to South African rule.

From the 1950s, the international community, through the UN and the International Court of Justice (ICJ) exerted pressure on the South Africa government to withdraw from SWA/Namibia. In 1966 The UN terminated South Africa's Mandate over the territory, and a year later the 11-member **UN Council for South West Africa** was established. This body gave much non-military support to SWAPO, such as establishing education programmes, throughout the struggle. However, it was not until 1971 that South Africa's occupation of SWA/Namibia was declared illegal by the ICJ.

The first clash between SWAPO soldiers and the South African Police took place at Ongulumbashe in northern Namibia on 26 August 1966. South Africa co-operated closely with the Portuguese colonial authorities in Angola and SWAPO was, therefore, initially forced to operate from Zambia, more than 1000km (624 miles) from its most important support base.

Despite this drawback, not only did SWAPO succeed in mobilizing the masses in Namibia, but in the early 1970s it became clear that the South African Police could no longer cope with the situation and in April 1973 responsibility for counter-insurgency was taken over by the South African Defence Force (SADF). The conflict, mainly fought on Namibia's northern borders, was to continue until April 1989.

After Angolan independence in 1975 SWAPO based itself in that country. To complicate matters, Angola was fighting its own civil war between UNITA, backed by

Opposite: *Youngsters enjoy a game of soccer in Katutura, a township created under apartheid rule in the late 1950s. Jobs are scarce in Namibia, and many of these youths will unfortunately join the ranks of the unemployed.*

THE INTERNATIONAL COURT OF JUSTICE (ICJ)

South Africa's dispute with the UN over Namibia featured prominently in the ICJ over more than two decades. **1950:** ICJ says that South Africa is under no obligation to conclude a new trusteeship agreement with UN, but must accept the supervision of UN General Assembly. **1955 and 1956:** ICJ states that UN General Assembly is empowered to supervise South Africa's administration of SWA/Namibia. **1960:** Ethiopia and Liberia institute proceedings against South Africa at the ICJ, charging it with violating its Mandate. **1962:** South Africa challenges the jurisdiction of the Court over its affairs without success. **1966:** ICJ rejects claims by Ethiopia and Liberia. **1971:** South Africa's continued presence in Namibia is declared illegal by the ICJ.

Above: *A colourful street mural in Katutura boldly expresses support for Sam Nujoma, Namibia's first president.*

South Africa, and the MPLA, supported by the Soviet Union and Cuba. The SADF invaded Angola in 1975.

Meanwhile, South Africa convened the internal parties in Namibia in Windhoek to draw up a constitution. This was the **Turnhalle Conference** of 1975, and the draft constitution that it produced in 1977, with the approval of South Africa, was rejected by the UN Security Council. South Africa went ahead with general elections in Namibia in 1978. SWAPO called for an election boycott, and the UN Security Council declared the whole process invalid. Nonetheless, the Democratic Turnhalle Alliance, who won the majority of the votes in the election, governed the country until 1983. A conference of internal parties, known as the **Multi-Party Conference** (MPC), was then convened in September 1983 and in May 1985 the MPC held talks with SWAPO in Lusaka. However, no agreement was reached and, on request of the internal parties, on 17 June the **Government of National Unity** was installed in Windhoek. Two days later the UN Security Council condemned the South African government's action towards determining the future political development of Namibia unilaterally and declared the action illegal.

Throughout this period when South Africa tried to install a pro-South Africa government in Windhoek diplomatic efforts for a negotiated settlement continued. In April 1978 South Africa accepted the proposals of the Western Contact Group for a settlement of the Namibian dispute. **Resolution 435** was adopted by the Security Council in September 1978. However, given the wide support SWAPO enjoyed, South Africa realized that the organization would win an internationally supervised election and so dragged its heels to buy more time in the hope of defeating SWAPO militarily.

To understand the processes that ultimately led to Namibian independence it is necessary to consider the security situation in southwestern Africa during the late 1980s. South Africa became increasingly involved in the conflict between the Angolan government (MPLA) and UNITA. If the latter was defeated, SWAPO would be in a position to open the battlefront eastwards by several hundred kilometres. The biggest land battle fought in this conflict, and, indeed, ever fought in Sub-Sahara Africa, took place in October 1987 at the Lomba River. The SADF forced the opposing forces to fall back west of the Cuito River. Ironically, the bloody battle that raged at **Cuito Cuanavale** and resulted in a stalemate proved to be the turning point in the search for a peaceful solution. The parties involved realized that peace could only be achieved through negotiations and not through the barrel of a gun, as an escalation of the war would demand a high price, economically and in human lives.

The ongoing **diplomatic negotiations** resulted in an agreement on a new initiative for Namibia's independence between South African Foreign Minister Pik Botha and the United States Assistant Secretary of State for African Affairs Chester Crocker in Geneva, March 1988. Several high-level meetings later the **trilateral agreement** was signed by Angola, Cuba and South Africa in New York, 22 December 1988. It made provision for the phased withdrawal of an estimated 50,000 Cuban troops from Angola and the implementation of Resolution 435 in Namibia under the supervision of the UN Secretary-General, assisted by UNTAG.

UNTAG

The United Nations Transition Assistance Group (UNTAG) was established in accordance with Resolution 435 to assist the Special Represen-tative of the UN Secretary-General to supervise and control free and fair elections for a Constituent Assembly that would be responsible for drawing up a Constitution. The civilian component of UNTAG over-saw all aspects of the electoral process, while 500 police monitors supervised the proper maintenance of law and order. The military component of 4475 soldiers from 21 countries was responsible for monitoring the cessation of hostilities, and for supplying logistical support, communication and supplies for UNTAG's countrywide network.

Below: *UNTAG supervised the registration of voters for democratic elections in 1989.*

Above: *Queen Elizabeth II, seen here with President Nujoma, arrives for a state visit in 1991.*

BIRTH OF A NATION

5 August 1988: Geneva Protocol for implementation of Resolution 435 set.
22 December 1988: Tripartite Agreement signed.
1 April 1989: Implementation of UN Resolution 435.
November 1989: Elections take place. SWAPO wins a 56.5% majority
9 February 1990: Constitution, drawn up by Constituent Assembly, adopted.
21 March 1990: Independence celebrations.
1 March 1994: Reintegration of Walvis Bay enclave and offshore islands.

Within hours of the implementation of **Resolution 435** on 1 April 1989 the process was nearly derailed when heavily armed SWAPO forces crossed from Angola into northern Namibia. South African troops were redeployed, and in the clashes that followed 305 SWAPO and 27 South African soldiers were killed. A historic meeting at Mount Etjo Safari Lodge on 8 and 9 April between representatives of Angola, Cuba and South Africa led to the **Mount Etjo Declaration** that brought the implementation of Resolution 435 back on track.

Another of UNTAG's tasks was to ensure the return of thousands of Namibians who went into exile during the liberation struggle. The **repatriation of refugees** got under way on 12 June 1989, and by the end of September of that year, 42,736 Namibians were resettled, mainly from Angola and Zambia.

More than 97% of the 701,483 registered voters cast their ballots in the UNTAG-supervised election that took place between 7 and 11 November and was declared free and fair on 14 November. SWAPO won 56.5% of the vote, while the main opposition party, the Democratic Turnhalle Alliance (DTA), took 28.1% of the vote. Numerous overseas dignitaries, including Secretary-General of the UN, Javier Perez de Cuellar, were present at Independence Stadium on 21 March 1990 when the South Africa flag was lowered to be replace by the bright new Namibian flag and Sam Nujoma was inaugurated as the country's first democratically elected President.

In 1991 Namibia became a member of the Commonwealth. Diplomatic negotiations on the return of the **Walvis Bay** enclave and the offshore islands started soon after independence, and on 1 March 1994 the disputed territory was reintegrated into Namibia. Hifikepunye Pohamba was sworn in as Namibia's second president on 21 March 2005.

GOVERNMENT AND ECONOMY

Namibians elected their first **democratic government** in November 1989 under the supervision of UNTAG. SWAPO won 41 seats in the Constituent Assembly, while the DTA formed the official opposition with 21 seats, and five smaller parties claimed the other 10 places. A **Constitution** guaranteeing fundamental human rights and freedom was adopted on 9 February 1990 and is internationally viewed as both democratic and liberal. The powers of the State are divided between the Executive branch, the Legislative branch consisting of the 72-seat National Assembly and the National Council, and an independent judiciary.

The first years since independence have been characterized by political stability, and Namibia has often been hailed as a successful example of democracy in Africa.

To unify a nation that was torn apart by the liberation struggle, the government embarked on a policy of **national reconciliation**, while **affirmative action** has been implemented to ensure the advancement of the previously disadvantaged majority. To address inequalities between rich and poor, **sustained economic development** aimed at the eradication of poverty and the provision of better living standards is a national objective.

Since the liberation struggle was aimed at regaining the land dispossessed by the German and South African colonial administrations, the **redistribution of land** remains one of the most serious issue facing the government.

Infrastructure

The **road network** between the country's main towns is tarred, but minor gravel roads in rural areas, especially in the north, northwest and northeast, could be impassable after heavy rains.

Namibia has one of the highest **per capita incomes** in Africa (N$1842 in 2004), but incomes are unevenly distributed between black and white Namibians and urban and rural inhabitants. At independence 75% of the population lived on 43% of the land. As a result of the government's **land redistribution programme** and the acquisition of commercial farms by black Namibians, the unequal distribution of land is changing slowly but steadily. As a result of the harsh living conditions in the communal areas, **urbanization** has increased at a rapid pace since the late 1980s and numerous informal settlements have sprung up on the outskirts of Windhoek and other towns throughout the country.

Below: *Namibia's roads run as straight as arrows to far horizons.*

LINKING NAMIBIA TO SOUTHERN AFRICA

Prior to independence, Namibia's road system was oriented north-south, and the only major road links were with South Africa. However, since independence two major highway projects have been completed to improve Namibia's road links with other southern African countries. The **Trans-Kalahari Highway** not only links Namibia with Botswana, but also reduces the distance between Windhoek and Johannesburg by over 400km (248.5 miles). In the north-east of the country the **Trans-Caprivi Highway** provides a fully tarred road link between Namibia, Zambia, Zimbabwe and northern Botswana.

Rail services are provided by TransNamib, a government-owned corporation, and are predominantly freight-oriented. Passenger services are offered on all major routes. The major towns in the south, central and north-central regions, as well as Swakopmund and Walvis Bay on the coast and Gobabis in the east, are all served by the national rail network. Regular scheduled **bus services** between the country's major towns are provided by Intercape Mainliner.

Namibia has two **harbours**, Lüderitz in the south and Walvis Bay along the central Namibian coast.

The national **airline**, Air Namibia, operates regular international, regional and domestic passenger and freight services.

Agriculture

Namibia's relatively small formal agricultural sector is complemented by a large informal farming sector. Commercial agriculture is dominated by **livestock farming**, and beef accounts for about 80% of gross agricultural income. Cattle farming is centred in the eastern-central and central parts of the country, and the number of cattle fluctuates between 1.8 and 2.5 million. Most of the meat is exported to neighbouring South Africa, and Namibia

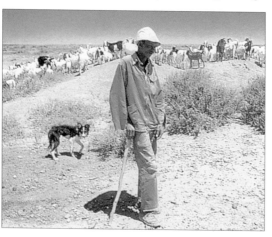

also has an annual quota of 13,000 tonnes of boneless beef under the Cotonou Agreement. **Small-stock** farming is practised in the sparsely vegetated, dry south, and the sheep population, reared for meat and karakul pelts, numbers between 3 and 4 million. Other agricultural activities are **dry-land crop production** of maize, **game farming** and the cultivation of crops such as cotton and vegetables under irrigation. Farming in the communal areas is **subsistence**-based and accounts for about 30% of the agricultural sector's contribution to the GDP. In the north the emphasis is on dry-land cultivation of **millet**, while in the east **cattle** farming dominates.

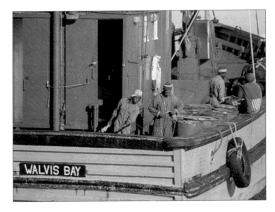

Fishing

Prior to independence, Namibia's rich fishing resources were plundered by foreign fleets and nearly depleted. As a result of the implementation of stringent conservation measures and the declaration of a 200-nautical mile Exclusive Economic Zone since then, however, the fishing resources have recovered remarkably.

Inshore pelagic fishing concentrates mainly on pilchards and anchovies, while large hake and horse mackerel stocks occur further **offshore**.

Lüderitz is the centre of the **rock-lobster** industry (see page 54). Due to over-exploitation and adverse marine conditions, annual catches decreased from 8600 tonnes in 1968 to only 130 tonnes in 1993–4, but stocks are slowly recovering and the 2002–03 quota was set at 400 tonnes.

The contribution of **fishing** and **fish processing** to the GDP varies as the industry is affected by unfavourable marine environmental conditions. In 2004 fishing and fish processing contributed 4% and 2.5% respectively to the GDP. The fishing industry is also one of the country's major employers.

Industry

Because of the relatively small domestic market and reliance on imports from South Africa, Namibia's manufacturing industry is poorly developed and its

Above: *Fishermen on a pilchard trawler at Walvis Bay, centre of Namibia's fishing industry.*
Opposite: *A herdsman watches over a herd of goats. Small stock such as sheep and goats are reared mainly in the arid south.*

MINING

Namibia's mining industry is the fifth largest in Africa and approximately 30 different **minerals** and **metals**, as well as **precious** and **semiprecious stones**, are mined in the country. Between 2000 and 2004 mining accounted for between 8% and 13.9% of Namibia's GDP. The most important mining products of the country are diamonds, uranium, copper, lead and zinc, while gold, silver, salt and a variety of semiprecious stones are also mined here.

MAJOR EXPORTS (2002)

- Diamonds
- Base metals, precious metals and minerals
- Food and live animals
- Manufactured products (e.g. fish, beer and soft drinks)

contribution to the GDP is a mere 10%. The most important activities are **meat** and **fish processing**, as well as the manufacturing and assembling of **mining, construction** and **agricultural equipment**. The informal manufacturing sector is also undeveloped, but has considerable potential. Special incentives have been created to encourage investment in the manufacturing section of the economy.

Energy

Nampower, the national power utility, is responsible for bulk **electricity supply** throughout Namibia. Since the capacity of the Ruacana hydro-electric plant on the Kunene River is insufficient to meet the country's growing demand for electricity, Nampower's grid is linked to the South African power utility, Eskom. This allows power to be exported or imported to and from South Africa. Prior to independence, the central and southern parts of the country had a well-developed electricity network, but the electrification of rural areas countrywide had been neglected. Many rural communities in the northern, eastern and southern regions have, however, been linked to the national electricity grid since independence. Plans to build a second hydro-electric scheme at Epupa, 120km (74.5 miles) downstream of Ruacana, were announced in 1990. Failure by the Namibian and Angolan governments to agree on the site of the dam has prevented the project from going ahead.

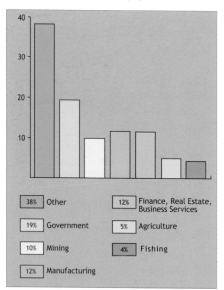

Gross Domestic Product (GDP) 1996-2001

- 38% Other
- 19% Government
- 10% Mining
- 12% Manufacturing
- 12% Finance, Real Estate, Business Services
- 5% Agriculture
- 4% Fishing

Social Services

Nearly 15% of the national budget is allocated annually to **health** and **social services**. Since independence the emphasis of the government's health policy has shifted from curative care to primary-health community-based health care.

Namibia has one of the best doctor : patient ratios in Africa, with one doctor for every 3650 persons, while the ratio of three hospital beds per 1000 people is also one of the highest in the continent.

THE PEOPLE

Namibia is a sparsely populated country with an average **population density** of 2 people per km² (0.4 sq miles). Population densities range from one person per 6km² (2.3 sq miles) in the arid south to nearly 12 persons per km² (0.4 sq miles) in the north. Around 60% of the country's 2 million people still live in rural areas.

Religion

Namibia is a non-secular state, with freedom of religion guaranteed in the Constitution. About 90% of the people are **Christians**, while small **Jewish** and **Moslem** communities are centred in Windhoek.

About 50% of the Christian population belongs to the three **Lutheran** churches. The **Dutch Reformed** Church ministers to Afrikaans-speaking communities. Other major denominations are the **Roman Catholic** Church, the **Anglican** Church and the **Methodist** Church.

During the liberation struggle, the **Council of Churches in Namibia** (CCN), formed in 1978 to promote ecumenical spirit among churches, played a leading role in highlighting the plight of the voiceless masses.

Language

On independence **English** became the official language of the country, but **Afrikaans** is still the *lingua franca* in large parts of Namibia, except in Caprivi where English is spoken. **German** is widely spoken in towns such as Lüderitz and Swakopmund, as well as in numerous businesses throughout Namibia.

The most commonly spoken indigenous languages are **Kwanyama**, a dialect of Oshiwambo, and **Ndonga**. Others languages spoken include **Herero**, **Damara/Nama**, four dialects of **Kavango**

TRADITIONAL RELIGION

Although 90% of Namibia's people are Christian, traditional religious beliefs and Christianity are still practised side by side, especially in the rural areas. **Ancestor cult** links the present social order with the living dead or ancestors. Nowhere is this better illustrated than at the annual Herero Day celebrations when the **Herero** pay tribute to their forefathers. The processions are preceded by various rituals and communication with deceased leaders.

Traditional religious beliefs are still fairly common among the **Himba** and **San** who have not been exposed to Christianity to the same extent as have people from other cultures.

Below: *Preparing for Sunday worship in a charming little church in the east of the Kavango Region.*

(Kwangali, Mbukushu, Gciriku and Mbunza), **Lozi**, **Setswana** and **San**.

Traditional Cultures

Namibia's people have mostly assimilated the Western culture imposed on them by the colonists, so there is little to be seen of traditional dress and culture, except in the remote parts of Namibia.

Above: *The traditional dress of Herero women is derived from the fashions worn by 19th-century missionary wives.*
Opposite: *The distinctive face of the Topnaars of the Lower Kuiseb River valley.*

Owambo

The mostly Westernized **Owambo** people constitute approximately half of the Namibian population and are divided into eight groups. More than 50% of the Owambo people are members of the two largest groups, the Kwanyama and the Ndonga.

San

During the early 1900s small groups of San **hunter–gatherers** were widely distributed throughout Namibia. Within less than a century, those who escaped extermination were either assimilated by other cultural groups or dispossessed of their hunting and gathering grounds.

Their demise was accelerated when farmers established themselves in their traditional areas, and in the late 1970s many of the men were recruited as soldiers by the South African Defence Force (SADF). When the SADF withdrew from Namibia, they were left destitute and many San, especially the younger generation, no longer knew the skills of hunting and gathering.

Today there are no San communities in Namibia living exclusively from hunting and gathering. Likewise, the skin aprons and other traditional clothing have almost completely been replaced by Western garb. The largest concentrations of San people live in the former **Bushmanland** and in **Western Caprivi**.

LANGUAGES

English is the official language of Namibia, but is the home language of only 0.9% of the population. Languages (home or first) spoken by Namibian people are:
- Owambo languages 50.6%
- Damara/Nama 12.5%
- Kavango languages 9.7%
- Afrikaans 9.5%
- Herero 8.0%
- Caprivi languages 4.7%
- San languages 1.9%
- English 0.9%
- Tswana 0.4%
- Other languages (including German) 1.0%

Herero

The Herero-speaking people consist of the Himba and the Tjimba of northwestern Namibia, the Herero of central and eastern Namibia and the Mbanderu in the east. Their economy, customs and religion are centred around **cattle**, while **ancestor worship** plays an important role in their culture and beliefs.

Colourful ceremonies are held each year to pay respect to their forefathers. At Okahandja, the 'Red Flag' Herero commemorate Maherero Day in August, and the Mbanderu or 'Green Flag' Herero honour their ancestral leader in June (*see page 40*). The 'White Flag' Herero pay homage to Chief Zeraua at Omaruru in October.

Himba

The Himba of northwestern Namibia, who are Herero people that chose to stay in Kaokoland when most of the Herero migrated to central Namibia during the 18th century, are the most exclusively **pastoral** of all Bantu-language speakers in southwestern Africa. Because of the isolation in which they live, even by today's standards, the Himba have until quite recently been little affected by Western influences.

The economic activity of the Himba centres around subsistence pastoralism, and prior to the devastating drought of the early 1980s they were one of the most wealthiest cattle-herder nations in Africa. They are semi-nomadic, moving constantly in search of grazing and water for their livestock.

While most Himba men have adopted some form of Western dress, women still wear their **traditional dress** of leather aprons, thongs and headdresses.

Topnaars

The Topnaars are one of nine Nama tribes, and are among the earliest inhabitants of Namibia. They live mainly in the **Lower Kuiseb River valley** and **Walvis Bay** areas,

A TRADITIONAL WAY OF LIFE

A striking feature of the **Himba** women is the paste of ochre powder and animal fat that they apply to their skin and hair both as protection from the harsh sun and as a cosmetic. Himba settlements are distinguished from those of the Herero by their circular and conical houses with a slight tunnel entrance; Herero houses are usually square or oblong with upright walls and roofs. An important feature of any Himba settlement is the sacred fire, which plays a central role in ritual and social functions at which the male head of the family officiates. Responsibility for the holy fire, however, rests with his mother, and after her death, his senior wife.

EKIPA BUTTONS

Ekipa buttons carved from ivory were worn by the **Owambo** women at the turn of the century as a symbol of wealth, and, as they are no longer made, they have become extremely rare. These pieces of jewellery are usually round or oval, with a diameter of 5cm (2in), and are some-times boat-shaped.

The ekipa had different patterns carved into them and were then rubbed with a powder derived from teak wood or the juice of aloes to accentuate the patterns. A leather thong was threaded through a hole drilled on the flat underside of the button, and it was then worn around the neck, the upper arm or at the back of the head; alternatively, the ekipa was fastened on to a wide belt.

Below: *Splendid catches are recorded on the Namibian coast.*

while a small community also lives at **Sesfontein**, about 500km (311 miles) north of these two areas. The Topnaars of the Lower Kuiseb live in 12 semi-permanent settlements along the northern banks of the Kuiseb River, and the community totals about 400 people.

Traditionally **pastoralists**, they used to supplement their diet by hunting, collecting seafood and gathering. Although the **!nara** (*see* page 9) is no longer their staple diet, this unusual plant still plays an important role in their economy, culture and diet. !Nara fields are owned by families and the property rights are hereditary. The kernels of the fruit are an important source of income.

Basters

The Basters of Namibia are a people of mixed stock, the descendants of the early white settlers at the Cape and Khoikhoi women. They settled in the vicinity of the hot springs at **Rehoboth** in 1870, having crossed the Orange River two years earlier to avoid confrontation with white *trekboers* who were encroaching on their territory.

Unlike in South Africa where the word 'baster' has a pejorative meaning, the Basters of the Rehoboth Gebiet, 90km (56 miles) south of Windhoek, are proud of their name. The main language spoken is **Afrikaans**. They are economically active in the building trade, as well as in commerce and industry, while small-stock farming is practised in the rural areas of the Rehoboth Gebiet.

Sport and Recreation

Namibia's coast is re-nowned for its excellent **angling** conditions, and in summer thousands of people flock to the coastal resorts here. The **hunting** of game to make *biltong* is a popular pastime during the winter months.

Football has the largest following in Namibia and is undoubtedly the national sport. During the season, from February to November, league and friendly matches are played every weekend, often on fields without any facilities.

Rugby, golf, tennis, as well as cricket, are also popular.

Athletics has attracted more attention after the excellent performance of Namibian sprinter Frank Fredericks in the 100m and 200m at the 1992 and 1996 Olympic Games and the silver medal won by Luketz Swartbooi for the marathon at the 1993 World Games.

Above: *Holiday-makers enjoy the sunshine outside Swakopmund's Strand Hotel. Namibia's leading seaside resort is noted for its restaurants.*

Food and Drink

Most eateries in Namibia offer a variety of continental, traditional German and South African fare and a truly Namibian culinary identity is still being developed.

Many restaurants include **game** on their menus. Kudu, springbok and gemsbok dishes are the most popular, while zebra, ostrich and other game specialities are occasionally offered. As Namibia is a major beef-producing country, **beef** steaks and dishes feature prominently on menus. A variety of **processed meats** and **sausages**, prepared in the traditional German style, are often served at cold buffets.

The traditional South African **braaivleis**, or barbecue, is a favourite for outdoor entertainment, while fresh line-fish like steenbras and kabeljou, as well as oysters from Lüderitz and Swakopmund, are popular **seafood** fare.

In this dry and hot country **beer** is the national drink. It is generally light and refreshing and brewed in the traditional German way as decreed by Duke Wilhelm of Bavaria in 1516. Also popular is a wide range of imported **German liqueurs** and *schnapps*, and a good selection of **South African wines** are available.

FOOD FOR THOUGHT

Biltong: spiced dried meat of Dutch origin.
Braaivleis: grilled (or barbecued) meal made outdoors.
Brötchen: German breadroll
Galjoen: popular firm-fleshed line fish.
Landjäger: German smoked beef and pork sausage.
Omajova: mushroom that grows on termite hills after the summer rains.
Schwarzwälder Torte: German Black Forest cake.
Sosatie: a South African version of the kebab.
Truffles: nut-flavoured fungus that grows underground in the Kalahari sands after rains.

2
Windhoek and Surrounds

Central Namibia is characterized by rolling hills which are deeply incised by numerous usually dry river courses that drain the inland plateau. Here Windhoek, Namibia's capital city, is sheltered by the Auas Mountains to the south and the Eros Mountains in the east. Situated at an altitude of between 1500m (4921ft) and 2000m (6562ft), the **Khomas Hochland** west of Windhoek derives its name from the Nama word 'Khomas', meaning hilly or mountainous terrain, and the German word 'Hochland', which refers to the plateau.

Farmers in the region surrounding Windhoek concentrate their efforts on beef production, while south of **Rehoboth** the wide open plains are ideally suited to small-stock farming.

For many visitors, **Windhoek** with its vibrant variety of African and Western cultures and old colonial German buildings is the starting point for a tour of well-known attractions in the country. Although many of the places of interest in central Namibia are easy day visits from the capital, they are also convenient as stopovers for travellers en route to destinations further afield.

Hardap Dam, some 260km (162 miles) south of Windhoek, offers excellent opportunities for game-viewing, bird-watching, freshwater angling and water-sports, and is a popular place to stop on a trip to the south. To the north of the capital, the resort of **Gross Barmen**, centred on a thermal spring, offers a pleasant break for travellers, while at **Okahandja** the colourful annual processions are a main attraction.

CLIMATE

Summers here are **hot** with daily highs of over 28°C (82°F) between October and February; evenings are usually cooler. **Winter** days are **milder**, with maximum and minimum means of 20°C (69°F) and 6°C (43°F) in July, but early mornings and evenings are crisp with occasional **frost**.

Windhoek's average annual **rainfall** is 365mm (142in); Mariental has a mean of 210mm (8in). Two-thirds falls between January and March, generally as violent **thunderstorms**.

Opposite: *Looking down Independence Avenue.*

Windhoek Area

WINDHOEK

Although Windhoek has an estimated population of approximately 240,000, you are likely to get the initial impression that the city is even smaller. This is because Windhoek lies in a wide valley with its suburbs tucked away in the surrounding hills. It is on account of this undulating terrain that the airport is located 45km (28 miles) from the city centre.

City Walks **

The **Aloe Trail**, an easy one-way ramble of about one hour along the ridge that separates the Klein Windhoek Valley from the city centre, offers a good perspective of the layout of Windhoek. You can set off from either the notice board below the water tower in Sinclair Street or at the crest of the ridge in Orban Street. Much of the natural vegetation on the route is still intact, and the aloes, Windhoek's emblem, are a delight in winter when they flower.

Towards the end of the 19th century, when the Germans settled here, the area with its springs was already popular with the Oorlam Afrikaners and the Herero. Stone Age tools about 5000 years old and fossilized elephant bones excavated in **Zoo Park**, a tranquil oasis in the centre of Windhoek, are evidence that the springs have attracted man and beast for millennia.

Walk down **Independence Avenue**, Windhoek's main thoroughfare, and you will notice the colonial German architectural influence. Three restored buildings in the street can be admired from under the palm trees in Zoo Park across the road. Here a plaque points out **Erkrath Building** (1913), **Gathemann House** (1913) with its steep roof and **Hotel Kronprinz** (1902).

Also in Independence Avenue, the **clock tower** at the intersection with Post Street Mall is an obvious landmark. It resembles the corner tower of the Deutsch-Afrika-Bank, built in 1908 but later demolished.

From Monday to Saturday the **Post Street Mall** bustles with shoppers at the morning street market where handicrafts ranging from wooden toys and rag dolls to Kavango woodcarvings and Zimbabwean malachite jewellery can be purchased.

Further down the Mall you can closely inspect the 31 **Gibeon Meteorites** on display. Although they could be mistaken for ordinary rocks, one has been sawn through to confirm their metal content. To date more than 77 meteorites have been recovered from the vicinity of Gibeon, south of Mariental.

The **Windhoek Information and Publicity (WIP)** bureau is in Post Street Mall.

KATUTURA

In 1959 the city's black people were forcibly moved to Katutura, a Herero word that means 'we have no dwelling place'. Thirteen people were killed in clashes with the Police on 10 December 1959, an event commemorated as **Human Rights Day**.

Housing in Katutura ranges from luxury homes to squatter settlements.

THE STATE MUSEUM

The State Museum in Robert Mugabe Avenue is housed in two buildings. If you are interested in archaeology and the cultural backgrounds of the indigenous people of Namibia, visit the **Owela Museum Display Centre** which is situated between Robert Mugabe Avenue and Lüderitz Street.

It is not only the design of the **Alte Feste**, which houses the other section of the State Museum, that is of interest; a variety of displays focus on the country's national symbols, the independence process, local household furniture, and implements used by the first European settlers.

Below: *The tall-steepled Christuskirche viewed from the imposing Tintenpalast.*

Guarding over the city centre is the almost fairytale **Christuskirche** (Church of Christ) in Robert Mugabe Avenue, completed in 1910 by the German Evangelical community as a monument to peace. Behind it is the **Tintenpalast** (Ink Palace), which was built in 1913 and now houses the Namibian Parliament, with its shady lawns and attractive gardens

Cross over the road towards the **Alte Feste** (old German fort), and you will pass the **Equestrian Memorial** which was unveiled in 1912 in memory of the Germans killed in the Nama and Herero wars of 1903–7. Strategically positioned by Curt von François in 1890, the Alte Feste is Windhoek's oldest surviving building.

Other imposing German colonial buildings include the **officers' house** (now the Bank of Namibia training centre), and the **old school building**, which now houses the museum staff, with its quaint tower.

Windhoek's Castles

Perched on the hill that separates Klein Windhoek and Windhoek are three 'castles'. They were designed by Willi Sander who was also responsible for Duwisib Castle (*see*

page 39). **Schwerinsburg**, initially a watchtower and a small tavern, was completed in 1914, followed by **Heinitzburg** and **Sanderburg** (built for Sander himself) in 1917. Heinitzburg is an upmarket hotel; the other two 'castles' are privately owned.

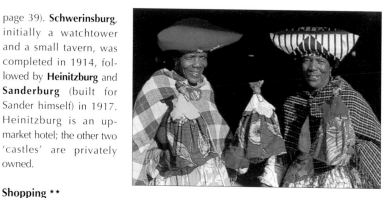

Shopping ★★

Ostrich-skin and buffalo-hide **leather goods** and **Swakara** jackets are very good buys here as prices are reasonable compared to what you would pay in Europe. Shops that sell leather and Swakara items are Pelzhaus Huber, Seelenbinder and Nakara in Independence Avenue.

Much of the locally handcrafted **jewellery** is inspired by the diverse Namibian landscape. Although most of the jewellers were trained in Germany, their work has an African flair and is not as heavy-looking as that produced in Europe. Agates, semiprecious stones from northwestern Namibia, as well as tourmalines and diamonds, are incorporated in the silver and gold pieces. Shops to visit in Independence Avenue are Adrian and Meyer, Canto Jewellers in Jack Levinson Arcade and Herrle & Herma Jewellers.

Gemstone collectors can browse through a number of shops – Rocks and Gems, Independence Avenue, and The House of Gems, Werner List Street. Take care, though, when buying gemstones from curio shops as you could be buying a stone imported from South America.

The **Namibia Crafts Centre** in the Old Brewery Building in Tal Street is the place to buy souvenirs such as African-style clothing and colourfully embroidered household goods, including cushion covers and tablecloths. Basketry, wood and stone carvings can also be bought at the Post Street Mall market and at the

Above: *Herero women display handcrafted dolls dressed in traditional garb.*

THEATRES AND ART GALLERIES

• The **Warehouse Theatre**, in the old brewery in Tal Street, usually stages cabarets and one-man shows.
• The **National Theatre of Namibia**, situated on the corner of John Meinert Street and Robert Mugabe Avenue, presents occasional cultural performances.
• The **College of Arts** in Fidel Castro Street has occasional music, ballet and modern dance performances.
• The **National Art Gallery of Namibia**, on the corner of Robert Mugabe Avenue and John Meinert Street, has a permanent exhibition of Namibian art.
• **Commercial galleries** selling local art include Artelier Kendzia, Volans Street, and the Omba Gallery in the Old Breweries Building.

bus terminus on the corner of Fidel Castro Street and Independence Avenue. The Bushman Art curio shop in Independence Avenue has an interesting variety of authentic Namibian **curios** and **karakul rugs**, while African Curiotique, Elephant crossing and Rogl Souvenirs, Independence Avenue, are also well worth a visit.

Above: *The green and pleasant landscape of the Daan Viljoen Game Park.* **Opposite:** *Liebig Haus, a relic of Namibia's German colonial past.*

GAME-VIEWING AND BIRD-WATCHING

Visitors will find a visit to the **Daan Viljoen Game Park** rewarding as the wildlife can be observed at fairly close range. Resident antelope include blue wildebeest, red hartebeest, kudu, eland, gemsbok, impala and spring-bok, and other mammals you may see are Hartmann's mountain zebra, warthog, chacma baboon, klipspringer, steenbok and rock dassies.

With about 260 bird species in the park, bird-watching can be rewarding too, and in summer you could spot up to 60 species. Look out for Monteiro's horn-bill, rockrunner and white-tailed shrike.

Daan Viljoen Game Park

This small game park, about 20km (12 miles) west of Windhoek along a tarred road, offers alternative over-night accommodation for visitors to the city. Although the bungalows are fairly basic, they are picturesquely situated on the banks of the reservoir formed by the Augeigas Dam. The park is popular with Windhoekers over weekends and on public holidays but on one of the walks you can enjoy peace and tranquillity.

There is a short circular game-viewing drive through the Daan Viljoen Game Park, but perhaps the best way to familiarize yourself with the range of flora and fauna typical of the undulating hills of the Khomas Hochland is to set out on foot and tackle either the 3km (2 miles) **Wag 'n Bietjie Trail** or alternatively the more strenuous 9km (5.5 miles) **Rooibos Trail**. The focal point of the first trail is the Stengel Dam where you could spot game, while magnificent views over the Khomas Hochland are a highlight of the longer route. The more fit may prefer to tackle the **Sweet Thorn Hiking Trail**, a two-day route over about 32km (20 miles).

Among the facilities at Daan Viljoen are an inviting swimming pool and a good restaurant which serves breakfast, buffet lunches and dinners, and there are also a number of picnic and camp-fire places for day visi-tors. Contact Namibia Wildlife Resorts in Windhoek for reservations and information.

Khomas Hochland

West of Windhoek the hilly highland plateau of central Namibia is traversed by three gravel-surface routes which lead down the **Gamsberg**, **Us** or **Bosua** passes to the Namib Desert. A day drive from the capital to the top of one of these passes and back will reward you with views of the seemingly never-ending rolling hills which abruptly drop away to the vast plains of the desert.

Of particular interest on the route via Daan Viljoen Game Park to the top of the Bosua Pass are Liebig Haus, about 42km (26 miles) west of Windhoek, and further on the ruins of Von François Fort.

Liebig Haus was built in 1912–13 and, although now rather ramshackle, it still creates an imposing scene besides looking rather incongruous. Features like the steeply pitched roof, which was designed to allow snow to slide off, and the solarium indicate that the house was typical of those built in Germany at the time.

Just as fascinating is the **Von François Fort** which was built in 1890 by Major Curt von François when he moved his headquarters from Tsoabis to Windhoek. Subsequently German soldiers guilty of drunkenness were sent to this outpost, hence it was given the name *Trockenposten* (meaning 'dry post').

HORSE TRAILS

You can explore the Khomas Hochland on horseback. **Farm Hilton**, about 65km (40 miles) from Windhoek, offers a guided 400km (248 miles) trail that leads down the escarpment and through the Namib to Swakopmund. The trail takes nine days to complete and has been described as one of the ten best adventure trips in Africa.

Above: *The attractive Rehoboth Museum.*

Although there are a number of guest farms that are closer to Windhoek, **Namibgrens Guest Farm** near the summit of the **Spreetshoogte Pass** is reached after a pleasant drive through the Khomas Hochland. Views of the Namib from the top of the pass are spectacular.

Rehoboth

The therapeutic thermal spring and an interesting museum are the attractions of this often bypassed town.

Less than an hour's drive (80km; 50 miles) south of Windhoek, you will pass the turnoff to Rehoboth's water storage dam, the **Oanob Dam**, shortly before entering the town. Construction was completed in 1990, and the reservoir has a storage capacity of 35 million m³ (1236 million cu ft). **Lake Oanob Resort** has fully equipped self-catering chalets, a floating restaurant, camping sites and picnic spots for day visitors. The resort's marina has a swimming pool and offers a variety of water sports – boating, canoeing, water-skiing and aqua-biking.

The **Basters**, a mixed race of Khoikhoi and Dutch people who originated in South Africa, settled around the hot-water spring here in 1870. The history of the Baster people is well illustrated in the **Rehoboth**

Museum which was once the home of the town's first postmaster. Other displays feature aspects of the life of the former San inhabitants of the area. By prior arrangement you can also visit an archaeological excavation of an **open-air burial site** of Late Iron Age people close by.

MARIENTAL AND SURROUNDS

Just north of Mariental a signpost indicates the turnoff to **Stampriet**, 52km (32 miles) on along a tarred road. The strong artesian waters which were discovered here in 1910 irrigate a variety of crops, and the area is renowned for its watermelons, sweet melons and grapes.

From here a gravel-surface road follows the course of the Auob River, ending abruptly at **Mata Mata** on the South African border. This entrance gate to the Kalahari Gemsbok National Park has been closed since independence. The Namibian Cabinet agreed in 2005 to the reopening of Mata Mata, but gave no indication of when it will be opened. It is advisable to check with South African National Parks in South Africa before considering this route.

Situated about halfway between Windhoek and Keetmanshoop is **Mariental**, the administrative hub of the Hardap region and an important agricultural centre. It has little to offer tourists, but worthy of mention are the nearby Hardap Recreation Resort and the luxury **Intu Afrika Game Lodge**, which offers game-viewing among the rolling dunes of the Kalahari.

Below: *A devout member of Namibia's 50,000-strong, Afrikaans-speaking Baster community. Her forefathers arrived from the Cape in 1870 to settle in and around Rehoboth, to the south of Windhoek.*

Hardap Recreation Resort

The focal point of the resort is the 25km² (10 sq miles) reservoir of the **Hardap Dam**, Namibia's largest. It was completed in 1962 by constructing a wall 865m (2838ft) in length between two outcrops along the course of the Fish River. The spectacular Fish River Canyon is further downstream.

BIRD-WATCHING AT HARDAP

Many of the 300 bird species recorded in the **Hardap Recreation Resort** and **Game Reserve** can be observed at the dam where up to 800 white pelicans (one of the largest breeding colonies in Namibia), over 20 species of waders and a large number of heron and duck species, as well as the occasional pink-backed pelican, have been recorded.

The rolling hills and plains of the game reserve attract ostrich and bustard, as well as several lark, thrush and chat species, while the cliffs around the dam provide an ideal habitat for rock pigeons, rosy-faced lovebirds and Bradfield's swifts.

The dam supplies water to Mariental and the 40-odd smallholdings of the Hardap Scheme where a variety of crops are cultivated under irrigation.

The large reservoir is especially popular with water-sport enthusiasts, and at weekends large numbers of people flock here to enjoy waterskiing, sailing and windsurfing. Freshwater angling is another popular pastime, and there are several fishing spots with facilities for day visitors along the northern shore of the dam, which is stocked with eight species of freshwater fish.

The rest camp on the cliffs offers a choice of accommodation ranging from bungalows to dormitories and two-bed rooms, as well as camping and caravan sites. A special feature of the resort is the restaurant with its commanding view over the dam where visitors are served breakfast, buffet lunches and dinners, while the swimming pool is much appreciated on hot summer days. Contact Namibia Wildlife Resorts in Windhoek for reservations and information.

Game which can be found in the not often visited **Hardap Game Reserve** in the southwestern section of the resort includes gemsbok, springbok, kudu, red hartebeest, steenbok and Hartmann's mountain zebra. There is also a possibility that you may encounter the southernmost population of black rhino in Namibia. Hikers in particular should watch out for this potentially dangerous animal when undertaking the 9km (5.5 miles) or 15km (9 miles) self-guided circular trail.

Maltahöhe and Duwisib Castle

Travel westwards from Mariental and you will reach the small settlement of **Maltahöhe** after about an hour's drive along a tarred road. Situated on the edge of the Schwarzrand plateau, the town lies at the centre of an important karakul farming district. It is within easy reach of attractions such as Duwisib Castle, as well as Sesriem and Sossusvlei, and is a convenient stopover between Lüderitz and Swakopmund. The **Maltahöhe Hotel**, with its quaint bar, has been a watering hole for travellers since 1907.

The stone fortress **Duwisib**, 70km (43 miles) south of Maltahöhe, seems altogether misplaced in its almost desolate setting. It is constructed from red-brown stone quarried close by and blends in extremely well with the surrounding hills, so well that you usually notice it only when you reach the signpost for the turnoff. There is a campsite with ablutions and camp-fire places under shady camel thorn trees in the grounds below the castle. Contact Namibia Wildlife Resorts in Windhoek for reservations and information.

Above: *The romantic German colonial fortress-like former home of Captain Von Wolf, Duwisib Castle, has been restored.*

Opposite: *The limpid waters of Hardap Dam, northwest of Mariental, are a popular venue for anglers and watersport enthusiasts.*

HERERO FOREFATHERS

Hosea Kutako (1872–1970): Herero chief, strongly opposed to South African occupation, was the first to petition the UN (in 1946). Committed to unity among Namibia's people, he chose to be buried near Jonker Afrikaner (c1785–1861), enemy of the Herero people, rather than in the cemetery where Tjamuaha, Maherero and Samuel Maherero were laid to rest.

Clemens Kapuuo (1923–78): succeeded Kutako, and became first President of Democratic Turnhalle Alliance (DTA) in 1977. He was assassinated in Windhoek, 27 March 1978.

MURDER HILL

A small outcrop along the B2 bypassing Okahandja serves as a reminder of the numerous battles fought between the Oorlam Afrikaners and their allies and the Herero. The vast herds of cattle owned by the Herero were irresistible to the Afrikaners who conducted numerous raids against the Herero despite peace agreements of 1842 and 1870. About 700 followers of the Herero Chief, Kahitjene, were killed in the battlle at this outcrop in August 1850. It later became known as Moordkoppie, or Murder Hill.

HERERO AND MBANDERU PROCESSIONS

Situated only 70km (43 miles) north of Windhoek, this quiet town at the junction of the routes to Swakopmund at the coast and the Waterberg and Etosha in the north is usually bypassed. The town grew around a mission station which was established at a spring here in 1850.

The Herero people have deep roots in **Okahandja** and each year on a Sunday towards the end of August the town is a blaze of colour with a procession of the **Red Flag Herero**. This is an occasion not to be missed if you are in the area at the time. Women in their brilliant red traditional Victorian-style dresses and headgear and men in military-style uniforms honour their forefathers Tjamuaha, Maherero and Samuel Maherero at a communal grave and then continue to the graves of Hosea Kutako and Clemens Kapuuo, which are next to each other. To confirm the date for the procession, contact the Okahandja Municipality.

Another colourful event on the Herero calendar is the procession of the **Green Flag Herero**, or Mbanderu, who pay homage to their forefather, Kahimemua Nguvauva, on the weekend closest to the anniversary of his execution on 13 June 1896.

Kavango woodcarvers have established markets on the southern and northern sides of the town and it is worth stopping here if you are souvenir hunting.

Gross Barmen

Although often crowded over weekends, the resort, built around a **thermal spring** 24km (15 miles) west of Okahandja, is nonetheless worth a visit on your travels to the north. The spring is known for its therapeutic qualities and visitors have a choice of relaxing in the indoor thermal pool, where the water temperature is about 41°C (106°F), or the outdoor pool, which is 12°C (54°F) cooler. Those suffering from heart or kidney complaints should use the pools in moderation.

It is not only the thermal spring that is of interest here; the surroundings are worth exploring on foot. West of the dam, close to a lone palm tree, look out for the almost vanished **ruins** of a church and mission house which date back to 1871. The rocky outcrops and reedbeds surrounding the dam could prove rewarding for bird-watching, so have a pair of binoculars handy.

Accommodation at the Gross Barmen Resort ranges from the luxury of air-conditioned chalets to campsites. Facilities include a restaurant which serves breakfast, buffet lunches and dinners, a shop and a petrol station. Contact Namibia Wildlife Resorts in Windhoek for reservations and information.

GROSS BARMEN MISSION STATION

The first mission station for the Herero people in Namibia was built around a spring in a tributary of the Okahandja River, 24km (15 miles) southwest of Okahandja. Originally known as Otjikango, meaning 'a spring flowing weakly through rocky ground', it was renamed Neu Barmen after the headquarters of the Rhenish Missionary Society in Barmen, Germany. It was later called Gross Barmen. The mission station was closed in 1890 because of fierce clashes between the Herero and the Oorlam Nama. Today, the ruins of the church and mission house are hardly visible.

Opposite: *In August each year, thousands of Herero gather in Okahandja to pay homage to their forefathers who are buried here.*
Left: *The Gross Barmen thermal spring resort, to the west of Okahandja.*

Windhoek and Surrounds at a Glance

Cool, dry winter months of **May** to **September** are best. Expect high temperatures and heavy downpours (the three gravel-surfaced roads to Namib are sometimes impassable) in summer, **November** to **March**. During **school holidays** (December/January) some restaurants and smaller shops in Windhoek are closed as locals head for the coast on holiday.

Hosea Kutako International Airport is approximately 45km (28 miles) east of city. For regular flights to and from Johannesburg, Cape Town, Luanda, Maun, Victoria Falls and Frankfurt, contact Air Namibia, tel: (061) 2996444, fax: 2996168.
Eros Airport, just 4km (2.5 miles) from the city centre, offers regular domestic flights countrywide. A regular **transfer service** between the airport and the city centre is provided by Marenko Shuttle, tel: (061) 226331. Incoming flights are met by taxis. Luxury **coach services** between Walvis Bay, Swakopmund and Johannesburg, Cape Town or Victoria Falls via Windhoek are offered by Intercape Mainliner, tel: (061) 227847. Ekonolux also has a weekly service between Walvis Bay and Cape Town, tel: (064) 205935.

Windhoek is the centre of an excellent network of **tarred roads**. **Taxis** can usually be found at the rank on the corner of Fidel Castro St and Independence Avenue, or call Prime Radio Taxi, tel: (061) 272221. Many **car-hire** firms are represented in the city. In **Windhoek**, contact: Avis, tel: (061) 233166, fax: 223072; Budget, tel: (061) 228720, fax: 227665; Hertz, tel: (061) 256274, fax: 256649; Imperial, tel: (061) 227103, fax: 222721. At **Hosea Kutako International Airport**: Avis, tel: (062) 540271, fax: 540254; Budget, tel: (062) 540225, fax: 540251; Hertz, tel: (062) 540115, fax: 540117; Imperial, tel: (062) 540278, fax: 540046.
In Windhoek, book a **four-wheel-drive** vehicle (do it well in advance) with Avis, tel: (061) 233166, fax: 223072; Britz, tel: (061) 250654, fax: 250653; Camping Car Hire, tel: (061) 237756, fax: 237757.
Small **aircraft charter** and **Air Namibia** flights to Swakopmund, Walvis Bay, Lüderitz, Oranjemund, Ondangwa and Katima Mulilo leave from **Eros Airport**, 4km (2.5 miles) from city centre. Contact Air Namibia, tel: (061) 2996444, fax: 2996168; Desert Air, tel: (061) 228101, fax: 254345; Comav, tel: (061) 227512, fax: 245612; Westair, tel: (061) 221091, fax: 232778.

Windhoek
Hotel Fürstenhof, Romberg Street: close to city centre, tel: (061) 237380, fax: 237855.
Hotel Heinitzburg: elegant old castle, tel: (061) 249597.
Kalahari Sands Hotel: luxury hotel in city centre, tel: (061) 2800000, fax: 259806.
Hotel Safari and Safari Court Hotel: 4km (2.5 miles) from city, tel: (061) 2986000, fax: 235652.
Windhoek Country Club Resort: rural setting 7km (4 miles) from city centre, tel: (061) 2055911, fax: 252797.
Pension Steiner: small, with private bathrooms, tel: (061) 222898, fax: 224234.
Villa Verdi: small but stylish pension near city centre, tel: (061) 221994, fax: 222574.

Mariental
Kalahari Anib Lodge, near Mariental: magnificent Kalahari scenery, tel: (063) 230066.
Intu Afrika Game Lodge: luxury accommodation, game drives, tel: (061) 248741.

Rehoboth
Lake Oanob Resort: chalets on Oanob Dam, watersports, tel: (062) 522370, fax: 524112.

Heja Game Lodge, midway between the city and airport; air-conditioned rooms, restaurant overlooking dam, game-viewing drives, tel: (061) 257151.

Windhoek and Surrounds at a Glance

Namibgrens Guest Farm, near Spreetshoogte Pass: magnificent views of the Namib, good hiking trails, tel: (062) 572021.

Windhoek
There are dozens of restaurants and coffee shops in Windhoek. Some good ones to try are:
Café Schneider, Jack Levinson Arcade: popular for light lunches, tel: (061) 226304.
Café Zoo, in Zoo Park: enjoy terrace dining with an innovative menu, tel: (061) 223479.
Hotel Fürstenhof, Romburg Street: excellent cuisine and service, tel: (061) 237380.
Joe's Beer House, 160 Nelson Mandela Avenue: open-air eatery, lots of atmosphere, tel: (061) 232457.
Gathemann, Independence Avenue: Excellent Namibian and continental cuisine, tel: (061) 223853.
Sardinia, Independence Avenue: excellent pizzas and pastas, tel: (061) 225600.

PARKS AND RESORTS
There are restaurants at Daan Viljoen, Reho Spa, Hardap and Gross Barmen.

For **safaris** from Windhoek (to destinations in Namibia and other regions in southern Africa), call Namib Travel Shop, tel: (061) 274500, 225178, fax: 239455.
Windhoek City tours and other day tours, including the **Gamsberg Trail**, conducted by Pack Safari, tel/fax:(061) 275800. **Guided horse trails** offered by Farm Hilton, tel: (061) 250764. Tours to **Sossusvlei**, **Etosha** and **Fish River Canyon** led by African Extravaganza, tel: (061) 263082. Hire **camping equipment** from Camping Hire Namibia, Windhoek, tel: (061) 252995. **Topographical maps** obtainable from Surveyor General, cnr Robert Mugabe Avenue and Dr AB May Street.

Automobile Association, cnr Independence Avenue and Fidel Castro Street, tel: (061) 224201, fax: 222446.
Namibia Tourism, corner Fidel Castro and Werner List streets, tel: (061) 2906000, fax: 254848.
Namibia Wildlife Resorts reservation office, 189 Independence Avenue, tel: (061) 236975, fax: 224900.
Windhoek Tourism Information Office, Post Street Mall, tel: (061) 2902092, fax: 2902203.
National Theatre of Namibia, tel: (061) 234633 or 374400.
Okahandja Municipality, tel: (062) 501051.
Rehoboth Museum, tel: (062) 522954.
Shops and galleries (Windhoek):
Adrian & Meyer, tel: (061) 236100; Atelier Kendzia, tel: (061) 225991; Bushman Art, tel: (061) 228828; Canto Jewellers, tel: (061) 222894; Herrle & Herma, tel: (061) 224578; Holtz – Safariland, tel: (061) 235941; The House of Gems, tel: (061) 225202; Nakara, tel: (061) 224209; Namibia Crafts Centre, tel: (061) 242222; Omba Gallery, tel: (061) 242825; Pelzhaus Huber Furs, tel: (061) 227453; Rogl Souvenirs, tel: (061) 225481; Seelenbinder, tel: (061) 224230.
College of the Arts, tel: (061) 374100.
State Museum: Alte Feste, tel: (061) 276817;
Owela, tel: (061) 276822.
Warehouse Theatre, tel: (061) 225059.
Windhoek Information and Publicity, Post Street Mall, tel: (061) 2902092, fax: 2902393.

WINDHOEK	J	F	M	A	M	J	J	A	S	O	N	D
AVERAGE TEMP. °F	74	73	70	66	61	55	55	61	66	72	72	75
AVERAGE TEMP. °C	24	23	21	19	16	13	13	16	19	22	22	24
HOURS OF SUN DAILY	9	9	8	9	10	10	10	11	10	10	10	10
RAINFALL in	3	3	3	1.5	0	0	0	0	0	0.5	1	2
RAINFALL mm	78	77	79	38	7	1	1	1	3	11	27	42
DAYS OF RAINFALL	11	11	11	5	2	1	1	0	1	3	5	7

3
Southern
Namibia

Southern Namibia is a vast, arid region with landscapes ranging from the desolate Namib in the west to the rolling Kalahari dunes in the east. The gravel plains merging with the horizon, rugged mountains and fascinating geological features will enchant you. Although stark and forbidding, the terrain is especially attractive during the early morning and late afternoon when pastel shades soften the landscape.

Keetmanshoop and **Lüderitz** are the only major towns in this sparsely populated region where distances between small settlements are great. The south is well suited to small-stock farming, and most of Namibia's sheep are found here – the black-headed Dorper are reared for mutton; karakul are bred for their pelts.

Most visitors explore central and northern Namibia, so tourism in the south is fairly low-key. Recently, however, several guest farms have sprung up in the region which offer visitors an opportunity to discover lesser known scenic attractions and the local way of life.

Attractions of the area range from spectacular geological features such as **Brukkaros**, an extinct volcano, to the awe-inspiring **Fish River Canyon**, one of the largest in the world, to the unique **quiver tree forests** near Keetmanshoop. Along the desolate west coast lies **Lüderitz** with its romantic history of diamonds, its ghost villages and beautiful German colonial architecture.

For the adventurous, there is the tough **Fish River Canyon Backpacking Trail**, or the challenge of canoeing on the **Orange River**.

CLIMATE

Summers are **very hot** in the southern hinterland, with highs of over 45°C (113°F). **Winter** evenings and early mornings can be as **cold** as 4–6°C (39–41°F). **Rain** falls in summer (except in the winter-rainfall area of the southwest), with an annual mean of less than 50mm (2in) in the extreme south and 100–200mm (4–8in) further north. The **cooler coast** has average highs of 21°C (70°F) in January and 17°C (62.5°F) in July. **Wind** is not uncommon; **mist** occurs 120 days a year.

Opposite: *The rugged grandeur of the spectacular Fish River Canyon.*

DON'T MISS

*** Fish River Canyon: among the largest in the world.
*** Kolmanskop: a fascinating ghost town near Lüderitz.
*** Orange River: a canoe trip through spectacular wilderness scenery.
** Quiver Tree Forests: unusually large concentrations of these tree aloes.
** Ai-Ais Hot Springs: a thermal spring situated in a strange lunar landscape.
* Lüderitz: a coastal town on the Diamond Coast with a distinctive German colonial atmosphere.

THE SOUTHERN HINTERLAND

South of Mariental, the road passes through what was formerly known as **Namaland**, an ethnic 'homeland' set aside by the South African government in the early 1960s for the Nama, a subgroup of the Khoikhoi people who speak the characteristic 'click' language.

Dominating the scenery to the east is a low plateau, the **Weissrand**, which stretches for over 100km (62 miles) southward. It derives its name from the white sandstone cliffs that cap the underlying shale and mudstone.

Mukurob

At the small settlement of Asab a signpost used to indicate the turnoff to **Mukurob** – one of Namibia's most popular tourist attractions until the 34m (111.5ft) high pinnacle toppled over during the night of 7 December or the early hours of 8 December 1988. The demise of this distinctive geological feature has been attributed to the gradual weakening of the narrow mudstone neck which supported a sandstone head about 12m (39ft) high – close to over a third of the height of the entire structure. It has also been suggested that the Armenian earthquake which registered strongly on the seismograph in Windhoek on the night of 7 December 1988 could have hastened its collapse.

All that remains of this well-known landmark which guarded the surrounding countryside for thousands of years are the base, a small remnant of the neck and the scattered remains of the sandstone head which was estimated to weigh about 637 tonnes.

Other names that were given to Mukurob were the Finger of God and the Afrikaans names *Vingerklip* (Finger Rock) and *Hererovrou* (Herero Woman), the latter because of

Southern Namibia

its resemblance to a Herero woman's face.

Brukkaros

Further south, **Brukkaros** dominates the landscape, and even from a distance the distinctly circular, rimmed shape suggests that it is an extinct volcano. Towering some 650m (2142ft) above the plains, the crater has a diameter of

Left: *Drought-resistant quiver trees, or koker-bome, stand sentinel in the rocky wastes of the southern hardveld tableland.*

about 3km (2 miles) and its floor lies about 350m (1148ft) below the rim. It was formed some 80 million years ago when large areas of Namibia were gripped by a final spasm of volcanic activity.

A well-defined path that starts where the road ends at the foot of Brukkaros leads into the crater, and the view from the edge is stupendous. Intrepid walkers should set aside a full day for this fairly strenuous ramble. Alternatively, hikers can camp at the base of the crater where basic facilities are available.

Quiver Tree Forests and Giant's Playground ★★

The **quiver tree forests** at Garas and the farm Gariganus, a few kilometres from Keetmanshoop, are worth a detour. These aloes usually grow singly, or in small clumps, but here they can be found among the black dolerite outcrops, forming unusually dense concentrations. Some of the large specimens are up to 5m (16ft) high and their age is estimated at between 200 and 300 years.

Close to Gariganus is the **Giant's Playground**, where visitors can have a close-up look at the amazing forces that shaped southern Namibia millions of years ago. Numerous large boulders are stacked on top of one another, and as you make your way through them you almost expect to be confronted by a giant. These large

---

THE QUIVER TREE

In Namibia the quiver tree, or *kokerboom*, is restricted to the arid western part of the country, occurring from the Orange River northward to the Brandberg. It is one of southern Africa's five tree aloes, and under ideal conditions it grows up to 9m (29.5ft) high. The fibrous trunk can measure up to 1m (3ft) in diameter at the base. During June and July dense masses of bright yellow flowers add a splash of colour to the landscape and provide nectar that attracts insects, birds and baboons. Sociable weavers often use these aloes as nesting sites. The distinctive quiver tree appears on the emblem of Keetmanshoop and is also depicted on the reverse side of the Namibian 50-cent coin. Its common name is derived from the San's use of the hollow branches as quivers for their arrows.

KARAKUL SHEEP

Southern Namibia with its low rainfall and sparse vegetation is ideally suited to karakul farming. The first of these sheep were imported into the country in 1907 to enable farmers to make better use of this arid area, and today Namibia is one of the world's major suppliers of karakul pelts. Also known as Namibia's Black Diamonds, these sheep are bred mainly for their pelts which are popular for fashion garments. **Swakara**, an acronym for South West Africa Karakul, is the trade name that is used at the Copenhagen Fur Fair. The industry has had mixed fortunes with the number of pelts exported annually decreasing from 3,7 million in 1972 to just under 60,000 in 2000. But it has since increased to nearly 104,000 in 2002. Black pelts are the most popular, although white, grey, brown and variegated are also produced. Italy and Germany are the major buyers, while Spain, Greece and the Nordic countries are among the alternative markets.

Above: *Keetmanshoop's rustic museum complex. In the foreground is a traditional Nama matjieshuis (thatched reed house).*
Opposite: *A touring party makes its way across the south-central Namib.*

stones are remnants of dolerite which intruded into the Karoo sediment some 180 million years ago. Subsequent erosion has removed the Karoo rocks, while weathering has removed the weaker of the dolerite rocks. The stacked boulders look a bit like warts on the landscape, hence it has been given the Afrikaans name *Vratteveld*.

Keetmanshoop

Keetmanshoop, the administrative centre of Namibia's largest region, Karas, is about 500km (311 miles) south of Windhoek. The Karas region covers 161,000 km² (62,162 sq miles), or nearly one-fifth of Namibia's total surface, and is named after the Karas Mountains southeast of town. Like many settlements in Namibia, Keetmanshoop developed around the site of a mission station. The historic **Lutheran Church** in Sam Nujoma Drive was inaugurated in 1895. It has been declared a national monument, and the attractive building now serves as a museum. Various displays depict the early history of the area. Especially interesting is the traditional Nama *matjieshuis* (a house made of thatched reed) in the church grounds. The museum is open Mondays to Fridays, 07:30–12:30 and 13:30–16:30 (16:00 Fridays).

Other historic buildings in the town include the old hospital in Second Avenue, which was completed in 1913 and is also known as the **Johanitter Haus**. The **Old Post**

Office in the town centre, between Hampie Plichta Avenue and Sam Nujoma Drive, was completed in 1910 and the prominent steep gable and the broad rectangular tower are conspicuous features. The **Southern Tourist Forum** has its offices here and will assist visitors with the latest information on the area. Opening times are Mondays to Fridays 07:30 to 12:30 and 13:30 to 16:30 (16:00 on Fridays). Another historic building is **Schützenhaus** (1907), headquarters of the oldest German Club in the country, in Gibeoner Street.

Gondwana Cañon Park

Situated to the east of the Fish River Canyon, the **Gondwana Cañon Park** covers 100,000ha (247,100 acres) of plains characterized by clumps of milkbush, granite outcrops and low mountains. The park's main attraction is the spectacular scenery, solitude and open spaces, and activities include guided nature walks and drives, scenic flights over the Fish River Canyon, and horse-riding. Accommodation is available at the Cañon Lodge, which nestles among the boulders of an outcrop near the viewpoints overlooking the Fish River Canyon. Another option is the Cañon Roadhouse, with its interesting collection of artefacts recalling modes of travel from a bygone era.

BETHANIE AND AUS

Add interest to the long journey between Keetmanshoop and Lüderitz by taking a detour to **Bethanie** where a mission station to serve the Nama was established by the London Missionary Society in 1814. National monuments in the small town include **Schmelen House**, the stone walls of which date back to 1814 and that now houses a museum, the adjacent **Rhenish Mission Church** complex, and **Joseph Fredericks House**, which was erected in 1883 by the Nama chief as a council chamber and dwelling.

Just outside **Aus**, about 210km (130 miles) west of Keetmanshoop, you can see the ruins of the **First World War camp** where over 1500 German prisoners of war were held from July 1915 to May 1919.

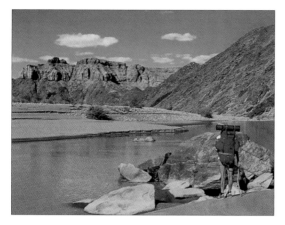

THE FISH RIVER CANYON AND AI-AIS ★★★

Namibia's most spectacular geological feature, the Fish River Canyon, is within easy reach of Keetmanshoop. Over countless millennia titanic forces in the bowels of the earth and the rushing waters of the Fish River have combined to create one of the largest canyons in the world – the upper section was formed by faulting of the earth's crust, while the lower canyon was eroded by the Fish River.

Several viewpoints along the sheer edge afford awe-inspiring vistas of the canyon, which reaches a depth of up to 549m (1800ft) and a width of up to 27km (17 miles). Its entire length is 160km (99 miles), but the most impressive section stretches from just north of the main viewpoint southward for about 65km (40 miles).

Early mornings and late afternoons are the best times to visit this attraction as then you can fully appreciate the changing kaleidoscope of colours at leisure. The small camp site of **Hobas** is just a 10-minute drive from the main viewpoint at the canyon so it is a convenient place to spend the night. A clump of trees provides much appreciated shade during the day for campers, and there is also a small swimming pool where visitors can cool off. Hobas is open throughout the year. Contact Namibia Wildlife Resorts in Windhoek for reservations and information.

A stopover at the **Ai-Ais** hot-springs resort in the lower reaches of the canyon is usually on the itinerary of visitors exploring the south. Situated on the banks of the Fish River, the resort is surrounded by scenery reminiscent of a moon landscape. Accommodation

---

FISH RIVER CANYON BACKPACKING TRAIL

Despite its reputation of being a tough trail, the Fish River Canyon Backpacking Trail is one of the most popular routes in southern Africa and each year several thousand hikers complete the 85km (53 miles) hike. Between the start at the northernmost viewpoint near Hobas and the end of the trail at Ai-Ais, hikers have to cope with ankle-twisting boulders, stretches of soft sand and temperatures of up to 40°C (104°F), even in mid-winter. The trail is only open between 15 April and 15 September, and the route should only be tackled by the fit as all food and equipment must be carried. Contact Namibia Wildlife Resorts in Windhoek for reservations and information.

ranges from fully equipped luxury flats to camping and caravan sites. Visitors have a choice of relaxing in the modern thermal hall or cooling off in the outdoor pool. Contact Namibia Wildlife Resorts in Windhoek for reservations and information.

South of Ai-Ais the Fish River continues to meander through the primitive landscape for 80km (50 miles) before joining the Orange River.

The Orange River ★★★

The Orange River forms a natural frontier with Namibia's southern neighbour, South Africa, for about 500km (311 miles). **Noordoewer**, a small settlement on the northern banks of the river, is the gateway for visitors travelling to Namibia by road from Cape Town.

Noordoewer is also the starting point of one of the most exciting adventures in Namibia – a **canoeing or rafting trip** down the Orange River. On the last part of its journey to the Atlantic Ocean this mighty waterway has carved its way through some of the most rugged terrain in southern Africa. The best way to explore this desolate and inaccessible landscape is to follow the course of the river downstream by canoe or raft. Trips last four to six days, the pace is quite relaxed and the mood is compan-

Opposite: *A hiker on the Fish River Canyon Trail. The cliffs to either side of the canyon slash up to 549m (1800ft) deep into the plains of southern Namibia. Some of the rocks here are 2600 million years old.*
Below: *The refreshingly green-garlanded Ai-Ais hot-springs resort.*

WILD HORSES OF THE NAMIB

West of Aus, on the road to Lüderitz, a signpost warns you to be on the lookout for horses. They are among the few groups of feral horses in the world, and the only ones to have adapted to harsh desert conditions. Mystery still surrounds their origin. Among several theories that have been proposed is one that suggests that they are descendants of domestic animals which ran wild from the Duwisib stud.

Their numbers depend on the available grazing, and range between 100 and 280. A viewing site has been built at Garub, the only water point in the area, which enables visitors to obtain close-up views of these rare wild creatures.

ionable. Stretches of tranquil water are interrupted by white-water rapids. No canoeing experience is required and if you are not up to a rapid, you can walk around.

Ai-Ais/Richtersveld Transfrontier Park

The Orange River forms the northern boundary of the Richtersveld in South Africa and the southern boundary of the adjoining Fish River Canyon Conservation Area in Namibia. The similarity of the geology, landscapes, flora and fauna of the two conservation areas resulted in the signing of a treaty on the establishment of a transfrontier park on 1 August 2003 by the Namibian and South African presidents. The park is managed jointly by South African National Parks and its Namibian counterpart. To encourage the free flow of visitors, the pont crossing at Sendelingsdrif will be recommissioned.

THE DIAMOND COAST

This barren, inhospitable region stretches from the Orange River mouth to just north of Lüderitz and extends about 100km (62 miles) inland from the Atlantic Ocean. Known as the forbidden territory, or **Sperrgebiet**, it is an area rich in diamonds and legend.

Oranjemund, at the mouth of the Orange River, is the centre of Namibia's diamond-mining industry and is unfortunately not accessible to tourists.

Lüderitz *

Lüderitz, the focal point of Namibia's Diamond Coast, is about 350km (217 miles) west of Keetmanshoop along a tarred road. There is much to do in and around this small coastal town so plan to spend at least two nights here.

The town has a notable German atmosphere which is created by the distinctive colonial-style buildings, several of which reflect the *Jugendstil* or Art Nouveau architecture of the turn of the century.

The imposing **Goerke House** on the slopes of Diamantberg (Diamond Mountain), built in 1909–10, is one of the diamond palaces that date back to the boom period of Lüderitz. It was first occupied by the Inspector of Stores, Hans Goerke, and later became the magistrate's residence. It is now used as a guest house for VIP visitors. It is open to the public from 14:00 to 16:00 Mondays to Fridays, and 16:00 to 17:00 on Saturdays and Sundays.

Opposite: *Canoeing on the Orange River past the Richtersveld National Park, which extends along the river's south bank.*
Below left: *German colonial buildings like the well-known Goerke House are a striking feature of Lüderitz.*

LÜDERITZ WATERFRONT

The N$30 million Lüderitz Waterfront Project forms an integral part of the harbour town's atmosphere and links the central business district to the ocean. It features a combination of public open spaces, market stalls for the craft manufacturers, shops, coffee shops, restaurants, apartments and offices. Harbour Square, with its natural rock features, granite cobbles and stone, offers stunning views over the harbour, with its fishing boats, diamond vessels, yachts and flocks of noisy sea gulls. A floating pedestrian pier extends for 60m (66yd) into the harbour from the square, and there is also a small tidal pool.

ROCK LOBSTER

Lüderitz has been the centre of Namibia's rock-lobster industry since 1921. These crustaceans (often incorrectly called crayfish) favour rocky reefs at depths ranging from less than 9m (29.5ft) to more than 20m (66ft), and the main fishing grounds stretch from near the Orange River to Oyster Cliffs, 150km (93 miles) north of Lüderitz.

The fishing season usually extends from 1 November to 30 April, and the lobsters caught must have a minimum carapace length of 650mm (25.5in). The legal restriction is an attempt to protect this valuable resource from being over-exploited. Annual catches declined from over 2500 tonnes in 1983 to 130 tonnes in 1993–4, mainly as a result of over-exploitation and adverse marine conditions, but the quota for 2000–03 was set at 400 tonnes.

Also dominating the skyline of Diamantberg is the **Felsenkirche**, completed in 1912, which has a commanding view over Lüderitz. It is open daily for 30 minutes at 17:45 (16:45 in winter), the best time of day for a visit as the beautiful stained-glass windows are then illuminated.

There are numerous other buildings worth viewing including **Kreplin House** (1909), a two-storey building with an asymmetrical façade, the houses in the **Altstadt** area in Berg Street, and the **Old Station Building,** which was completed in 1914. The small **Lüderitz Museum** in Dias Street is also interesting – opening times are 13:30 to 17:00), from Monday to Friday.

Spend a morning or afternoon exploring the **Lüderitz Peninsula**. A network of hard-surface roads is suitable for ordinary cars, but a word of caution – if you leave the road you not only risk getting stuck in loose sand, but will also do great harm to the fragile desert environment. Many delightful bays on the peninsula are worth a visit, as is the well-known **Dias Point** where Portuguese navigator Bartolomeu Dias erected a limestone cross on 25 July 1488 after he had succeeded in rounding the Cape of Good Hope. The **lighthouse** here dates back to 1910 and the **wooden bridge** was built in 1911 to provide access to the old foghorn tower that used to stand on Dias Point.

Although the water is cold, **Agate Beach**, north of the town, is an excellent place to go for swimming and surfing, and the long sandy beach is ideal for a late-afternoon stroll.

Shark Island in the bay is connected to the mainland by a causeway. A plaque near the end of the promontory was erected in honour of Adolf Lüderitz, the merchant of Bremen after whom the town

Left: *The monument to the merchant Adolf Lüderitz, founder of the settlement, on Shark Island.*
Opposite: *Lüderitz harbour is a thriving fishing centre and an outlet for the diamond diggings. The bay and its flanking coasts are a mecca for the bird-watcher.*

was named. The camp site here has one of the best views of any along the southern African coast, but it is often so windy that it is nearly impossible to pitch a tent. Contact Namibia Wildlife Resorts in Windhoek for reservations and information.

You can enjoy a different perspective of the Lüderitz Peninsula from the gaff-rigged schooner *Sedina*. It sets sail every morning, weather permitting, at 08:00, and on calm days continues to just off Halifax Island, giving you close-up views of the African (jackass) penguins on the island. Remember to wear suitable footwear and that it can be bitterly cold out at sea – warm clothing and a windproof anorak are essential!

Lüderitz is renowned for its sand-roses, which are crystals of gypsum and calcium sulphate salt that are also known as desert roses. They form under the sand in damp coastal conditions at Lüderitz and elsewhere along the Namib coast. You can buy specimens in shops at the town.

The Ghosts of Kolmanskop and Elizabeth Bay ★★★

Relics of the early diamond mining days can be seen at Kolmanskop, a few kilometres east of Lüderitz, and at Elizabeth Bay further south.

Following the discovery of diamonds at Grasplatz in 1908, a mining settlement sprang up at **Kolmanskop** and at the height of its growth more than 300 Germans

---

THE WATER SUPPLY OF LÜDERITZ

Obtaining fresh water at Lüderitz has always presented a problem. Early explorers got their supplies from the Nama who carried it from the interior in seal bladders and ostrich eggshells. In 1890 a seawater condenser was erected, but it could not cope with the demands of the growing settlement, and so an additional supply was shipped from Cape Town.

After the discovery of diamonds in 1908 water was at a premium and extremely expensive. When the railway line to Keetmanshoop was completed, this precious commodity was sometimes railed to the coast. However, it was as recently as 1968 that the water-supply problem was solved with the construction of a 113km (70 miles) pipeline from a borehole at Koichab Pan in the Namib Desert.

DIAMONDS

Diamonds are the largest contributor to Namibia's mining income and account for about 8% of the GDP. The industry is centred at Oranjemund, with satellite mines at Chameis and Elizabeth Bay further north and at Auchas, about 50km (31 miles) upstream of Oranjemund. Gem diamonds of high quality are mined and production averages about 1,500,000 carats a year. The alluvial deposits at Oranjemund are nearing depletion and increasing attention is being paid to offshore mining which accounts for over 60% of Namibia's total diamond production.

and approximately 800 contract labourers from the north lived here. When even richer alluvial deposits were discovered at Oranjemund, the fate of the town was sealed and in 1938 most of the mining equipment and workers were redeployed at Oranjemund. However, it was not until as late as 1956 that the last of the inhabitants finally left the abandoned settlement.

The sand dunes soon reclaimed what was rightfully theirs, burying some of the buildings of the once bustling settlement up to their roofs with sand, and giving the ghost town its distinctive character. Evidence of the lavish lifestyle of the miners can be seen in the beautifully decorated **Kasino** with its skittle alley and the remains of the splendid houses that were built for the mine manager and other senior officials.

Guided tours of Kolmanskop lasting approximately an hour are conducted from Monday to Saturday at 09:30 and 11:00, and also on Sundays at 10:00. Permits must be obtained prior to the tour from Lüderitzbucht Safaris and Tours in Bismarck Street before driving out to the old ghost town.

Elizabeth Bay, another deserted mining settlement, lies about 30km (19 miles) south of Kolmanskop. Mining started here in 1911, and the population of the town numbered about 200 Germans and 1200 contract workers from the north of the country. Operations finally came to a halt in 1948. Subsequently, a combination of lashing winds, salt-laden mists and chemical weathering have reduced the once busy settlement to a mere skeleton – on misty days the dark brown, weatherbeaten walls of the buildings, some eroded into a honeycomb pattern and others with large chunks of plaster stripped off by the wind, create a scene of utter desolation.

In 1989 it was decided to re-establish a mine at Elizabeth Bay, and its productive life span is expected to run until 2013.

Half-day tours of the ghost town at Elizabeth Bay are conducted by Ghost Town Tours. As diamonds are still being mined in the area, bookings (at Lüderitzbucht Safaris and Tours) must be made five working days in advance so that Police clearance can be obtained.

> ### THE BOGENFELS ARCH
>
> Perhaps the most remarkable feature of the bleak, often mist-wreathed southern Namib shoreline is what is known as the Bogenfels, a ruggedly sculpted arched rock that rises nearly 30m (98ft) above the Atlantic rollers. The arch – which is the highest coastal rock arch in southern Africa – once served as the terminus of a narrow-gauge private railway line that ran down the coast, linking the numerous small diamond mines of the pre-World War I era. Relics of one of the larger workings – a deposit discovered by the renowned prospector George Klinghardt – can be seen nearby.

Opposite: *One of Kolmanskop's once-splendid residences. In its heyday the diamond mining centre boasted shops, a hospital, a furniture factory, a lemonade and soda-water plant, four skittle alleys, a public swimming pool, and a grand hall complete with a theatre and an orchestra that played at tea dances. It is now a ghost town slowly being buried by the drifting sands of the desert.*
Left: *Bogenfels, a strangely sculpted rock arch on the southern Namib coast.*

One of the first people to real-
ize the potential of trade with
the people of the interior was
Benjamin Morrell, captain of
the American vessel *Antarctic*.
During his explorations along
the Namib coast in 1828, he
anchored off Ichaboe Island
and discovered the rich guano
deposits. When he returned to
the US Morrell tried unsuc-
cessfully to obtain financial
backing for his enterprises; by
the time his book *Narrative of
a Voyage to the South and
West Coasts of Africa*
appeared in 1844, exploitation
of the guano islands was
already in full swing.

Below: *Plumpudding
Island once played host
to 400 sailing ships and a
workforce of 6000.*

The Guano Islands

The coastline to the north and south of Lüderitz is dotted
with submerged reefs, rocky shoals and a string of
islands, the largest being the 90ha (222 acres) Possession
Island. The discovery of guano, a natural nitrate fertilizer
derived from accumulated bird droppings, on these
islands caused an unprecedented rush in the 1840s, and
within the first year 300,000 tonnes of guano were
stripped off Ichaboe Island and shipped to Britain. Guano
was collected from the islands for commercial purposes
until the end of 1992 when the tenders expired.

In 1861 Ichaboe was proclaimed British territory and
five years later 11 other islands were also annexed by
Britain. (However, numerous smaller islets and outcrops with names such as Dumfudgeon, Black Sophie
and Boat Rock were never proclaimed British territory.)
Sovereignty over the annexed areas was transferred to
the Cape Colony in 1874. Collectively known as the
Penguin Islands, some of them were given colourful
names such as Plumpudding and Roast Beef (or
Sinclair's), while others were simply descriptive names
(Long Island) or referred to specific mammals (Seal
Island) or birds (Albatross Rock). The islands and the
enclave of Walvis Bay
were reintegrated into
Namibia at midnight
on 28 February 1994.

Since these islands
are important breeding
sites for African (jack-
ass) penguins and other
sea birds, public access
is restricted. However,
you can enjoy good
views of the penguin
colony on Halifax
Island from Halifax
Point on the Lüderitz
Peninsula if you have a
pair of binoculars.

Southern Namibia at a Glance

Summers are very hot in the south of the country, so **May** to **September** is the best time to visit. **February** to **May** is pleasant on the coast, but it is quite cool throughout the year; expect mist year-round and also wind in **August**.

There are several scheduled **Air Namibia** flights a week to Lüderitz, tel: (061) 2996444, fax: 2996168. A regular **coach service** beween Windhoek and Cape Town and Johannesburg stops at Rehoboth, Mariental and Keetmanshoop. For in-formation contact Intercape Mainliner, tel: (061) 227847. For the budget traveller, TransNamib offers a regular passenger **train** service between Windhoek and Keetmanshoop, tel: (061) 2982032, and also a twice-weekly **bus** service between Keetmanshoop and Lüderitz, tel: (061) 2982032.

Tarred roads link Keetmans-hoop with Lüderitz and Noordoewer. **Gravel-surface roads** generally in good condi-tion and negotiable by car.

Aus
Klein-Aus Vista, just west of Aus: guided horse trails, hiking, guided tours to wild horses of the Namib, wide range of accommodation; tel: (063) 258021, fax: 258021.

Fish River Canyon Area
Cañon Lodge, near main viewpoint over Fish River Canyon: chalets nestling amongst rocks, nature drives and walks, horse riding, scenic flights over canyon; tel: (061) 230066, fax: 251863.
Cañon Roadhouse, near main viewpoint over Fish River Canyon: double rooms, charming bar and dining room, same activities as Canon Lodge; tel: (061) 230066, fax: 251863.

Keetmanshoop
Birds Mansions Hotel: tel: (063) 221711, fax: 221730.
Birds Nest Guesthouse: tel: (063) 222906, fax: 222261.

Lüderitz
Nest Hotel: tel: (063) 204000, fax: 204001.
Hotel Seaview Zum Sperrgebiet: tel: (063) 203411, fax: 203414.

Lüderitz
Ritzie's: seafood and steaks, tel: (063) 202818.
Penguin Restaurant, Nest Hotel: seafood restaurant with sea view, tel: (063) 204000.

For **Orange River canoe trips** contact Felix Unite, tel: (27 21) 6836433, fax: 6836488. Half-day tours of **Elizabeth Bay ghost town** and **Atlas Bay seal colony** run by Ghost Town Tours; day tours of **Pomona ghost town** and **Bogenfels rock arch** run by Coastaway Tours; apply at least five days in advance for Police clearance. For these tours and **yacht trips** book with Lüderitzbucht Safaris & Tours.

Lüderitz Museum, tel: (063) 202532. **Ministry of Environ-ment and Tourism**, Lüderitz, tel: (063) 202811. **Southern Tourist Forum**, Keetmans-hoop, tel: (063) 221266.

LÜDERITZ BAY	J	F	M	A	M	J	J	A	S	O	N	D
AVERAGE TEMP. °F	64	64	64	63	61	59	57	57	57	59	61	63
AVERAGE TEMP. °C	18	18	18	17	16	15	14	14	14	15	16	17
HOURS OF SUN DAILY	7	6	7	7	8	8	8	7	6	7	7	7
SEA TEMP. °F	68	66	64	63	63	59	59	59	59	59	61	61
SEA TEMP. °C	20	19	18	17	17	15	15	15	15	15	16	16
RAINFALL in	0	0	0	0	0	0	0	0	0	0	0	0
RAINFALL mm	1	1	2	2	2	3	2	2	1	1	1	1
DAYS OF RAINFALL	1	1	1	1	1	1	0	1	1	0	1	0
DAYS OF MIST/FOG	10	12	13	13	11	9	7	8	9	7	9	10

4
The Namib

The **Namib** is one of the most fascinating places on earth and home to a wide variety of desert-adapted plants and animals that are found nowhere else in the world. Stretching all the way from the Olifants River in South Africa to the southwestern parts of Angola, the most spectacular section of the desert lies between Lüderitz and Swakopmund.

The scenery varies from gravel plains with rocky outcrops in the south to the inhospitable sand sea of the central Namib and the flat gravel plains north of the Kuiseb River, which is choked by the encroaching dunes before it can reach the Atlantic Ocean at **Walvis Bay**.

Although entry to the Namib sand sea is prohibited because of the inhospitable terrain, many areas are still surprisingly accessible, even to ordinary cars.

Covering 4,976,800ha (12,298,170 acres), the **Namib-Naukluft Park** is the third largest game reserve in Africa and amongst the largest in the world.

Swakopmund, with its distinctive German colonial atmosphere, is a convenient base from which to explore the gravel plains and rugged Kuiseb Canyon in the **Namib** section of the park. It is also close to the **Walvis Bay Lagoon** and **Sandwich Harbour**, two of the most important wetlands along the west coast of Africa.

Contrasting sharply with the gravel plains are the rugged **Naukluft Mountains** with their crystal-clear pools, the spectacular dunes of **Sossusvlei** and **Sesriem Canyon** where the Tsauchab River has exposed millions of years of geological history.

CLIMATE

Though **coastal** temperatures are **moderate** – an average minimum of 9°C (48°F) in midwinter and maximum of 23°C (73°F) in **summer** – early mornings and late afternoons are often **misty** and cool. The mean annual rainfall is only 15mm (0.6in); precipitation is nearly always in the form of **fog**.

Further inland, daily temperatures are **moderate** in **winter** with a low of 5°C (41°F), but **highs in summer** exceed 35°C (95°F). The Naukluft Mountains get **summer rains** – about 195mm (7.6in) a year.

Opposite: *The searing sands at Sossusvlei.*

DON'T MISS

*** **Balloon Safari**: a bird's-eye view of the Namib Desert.
*** **Sossusvlei**: spectacular sand dunes of the Namib.
** **Welwitschia Drive**: scenic interpretive drive.
** **Swakopmund**: German colonial buildings.
* **Naukluft Mountains**: rugged scenery, day walks and hiking trails.

THE COAST

The 250km (155 miles) stretch between Walvis Bay and the Ugab River is the most accessible part of the Namib coast. Swakopmund, Henties Bay and Walvis Bay are popular holiday destinations, and excellent conditions for angling are a main attraction. Of interest is the salt-surface road which leads northward from Swakopmund.

Swakopmund **

Swakopmund with its distinctly German atmosphere (many locals speak German) is the country's most popular holiday resort, especially during the summer when thousands of Namibians flock to the coast to escape the intense heat of the interior. Just before you reach the town, along the B2 route, you will notice an old steam engine that is bound to rouse your curiosity. It came to a grinding halt here shortly after it was imported from Germany in 1896, hence the name ***Martin Luther*** after the Reformation leader who stated 'Here I stand, God help me, I cannot do otherwise'.

German colonial-style buildings dating back to the early 1900s still dominate the town. Notable are the **Swakopmund railway station** (1901) in Theo-Ben Gurirab Avenue, one of the finest in southern Africa, **Woermannhaus** (1905), built in *Fachwerkbau* style, in Bismarck Street, and **Hohenzollernhaus** (1906) with its high mansard roof, elaborate mouldings and statue of Atlas. The **State House** (originally called Kaiserliches Bezirksgericht) next to the **lighthouse** was finished in 1902 as a magistrate's court. It is now the residence of the President during the Cabinet recess in December/January.

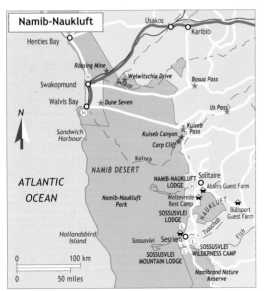

Take a ramble through the town to see the beautiful buildings, and visit the **Nambi I** office, corner of Sam Nujoma Avenue and Hendrik Witbooi Street, open Monday to Friday

Left: *Hohenzollernhaus, one of the many graceful colonial buildings of Swakopmund, a seaside resort surrounded on three sides by the vast Namib Desert. The nearby saltpans are famed for their variety of coastal and aquatic birds.*

08:30 to 13:00 and 14:00 to 17:30, Saturday 09:00 to 13:00 and 15:00 to 17:00, Sunday 09:00 to 13:00. Ask for the key to the **Damara Tower** of **Woermannhaus** at The Jetty gift shop at Am Ankerplatz for a view of the town. The **Swakopmund Art Association Gallery** in Woermannhaus is well worth a visit. It is open Mondays to Saturdays 10:00 to 12:00 and 15:00 to 17:00. The **jetty**, a good place to see the sunset, had to be closed in 1998 after it became unsafe, but plans are afoot to repair it. The iron pier, built in 1911–15, is 262m (859.5ft) in length, but was originally planned to be 640m (2,100ft).

Don't miss the mouthwatering German confectionery at **Café Anton** and **Café Treff**, or the variety of German breads – like Berliner (rye bread) and brötchens (bread rolls) – and cakes baked daily at **Putensen Backerei**.

The **Swakopmund Museum** in Strand Street is one of the most interesting in Namibia. Exhibits include a display of the early history of Swakopmund, archaeological and ethnological displays, a reconstruction of the old Adler Pharmacy and a fascinating collection of minerals. Daily opening times are 10:00 to 13:00 and 14:00 to 17:00.

Not to be missed are the **National Marine Aquarium** in Strand Street and the **Kristall Galerie**, corner of Tobias Hainyeko Street and Theo-Ben Gurirab Avenue, which houses the largest known crystal cluster in the world.

Although **Palm Beach** is safe for swimming, the water is usually too cold for anything more than a quick dip.

BEST BUYS IN SWAKOPMUND

• Karakul rugs and wall hangings from Karakulia.
• Handcrafted leather goods from Swakopmund Tannery.
• Paintings by local artists from Die Muschel and the Hobby Horse.
• A variety of gemstones from Stonetique.
• Handcrafted jewellery from African Art Jewellers and Engelhard Design.
• Namibian ethnic artefacts and colonial-period antiques from Peter's Antiques.
• Local first-day covers and stamps from Namib Stamps.

BIRD ISLAND

The large wooden platform built on Bird Island, about 7km (4 miles) north of Walvis Bay, is a familiar landmark along the coastal road. Built in 1930 by a Swakopmund carpenter, K. H. A. Winter, to collect guano from the thousands of birds that used to roost on the rocks at low tide, the platform originally measured 16m² (172 sq ft). It has been extended several times; the structure is now 17,000m² (182,988 sq ft) and is supported by no less than 1000 freestanding stilts. It provides a roosting and nesting place for thousands of Cape cormorants and smaller numbers of pelicans and other seabirds. Guano is collected during February and March, and is brought ashore by a motor-driven cableway. Annual production varies from 200 to 1000 tonnes.

Outings from Swakopmund

Earlier this century camels were widely used by the Police in Namibia as a means of transport; today they no longer serve this practical purpose. The **Camel Farm** about 12km (7.5 miles) east of Swakopmund, run by Mrs Elke Erb, offers the novelty of camel rides in the afternoon. It is best to make a reservation.

An interesting excursion from Swakopmund is a visit to the world's largest opencast uranium mine, **Rössing**, some 55km (34 miles) east of Swakopmund. Tours are conducted on the first and third Friday of the month. Book at the Swakopmund Museum.

The coast to the north and south of Swakopmund offers several opportunities to birders. Among the most noteworthy species to be seen here are the Damara tern, chestnut-banded plover, white pelican and a variety of summer migrants.

Long Beach and Dolphin Park

The coast south of Swakopmund is well frequented by anglers, and pelicans are often seen waiting patiently near fishermen for scraps of fish. The two modern resorts halfway between Swakopmund and Walvis Bay are very popular. The facilities at Long Beach include

Opposite: *The lagoon to the south of Walvis Bay is home to 80 different kinds of waterbird. These are among the 20,000 or so flamingoes that can be seen here at any one time.*
Right: *Camel rides are a popular attraction on a farm near Swakopmund. These exotic animals were used for desert transport in the early days.*

a fishing jetty, tidal pools, a trendy restaurant, various camp-fire places and camp sites. Dolphin Park, 3km (2 miles) further south, has been laid out like a park with a sports and a tidal pool, a waterslide, camp-fire places and a cafeteria.

Walvis Bay

Hemmed in by the Atlantic Ocean on the seaboard side and the golden-yellow dunes of the Namib further inland, **Walvis Bay** lies on a lagoon. The town is the centre of Namibia's lucrative fishing industry and also the country's only deep-sea port, so it is mainly a commercial settlement. It is also the largest producer of salt in Africa. The **Walvis Bay Salt Works** are situated to the south of the town, but they are not open to the public.

A familiar sight here is that of a flock of both greater and lesser flamingoes taking to the air from the lagoon, where they like to feed. The former species is taller, is white in colour and has a pink bill with a black tip; the latter is pink in colour and has a dark maroon bill.

Walvis Bay Wetlands ★★

The Walvis Bay wetlands, comprising the lagoon, salt works and western shores, are among the 10 most important coastal wetlands in Africa and supports up to 161,000 birds during summer and up to 68,000 in winter. Among the most common Palaearctic migrants are curlew sandpipers, sanderlings and little stints, while greater and lesser flamingoes account for more than 90% of the intra-African migrants. Low tide is generally the best time for bird-watching.

A novel way of exploring the lagoon is to join a **sea kayak tour** offered by Jeanne Meintjies of Eco-Marine

HISTORY OF WALVIS BAY

12 March 1878: port and surrounding country proclaimed British territory.
7 August 1884: port and settlement declared part of Cape Colony.
31 May 1910: incorporation of Walvis Bay into Union of South Africa.
30 September 1922: Walvis Bay placed under control of Administration of South West Africa.
31 August 1977: administration of Walvis Bay reverts back to Cape Province.
21 March 1990: independent Namibia's Constitution becomes effective, but South Africa still maintains sovereignty over Walvis Bay and offshore islands.
1 November 1992: joint administration of territory by Namibia and South Africa established.
1 March 1994: finally, Walvis Bay enclave and offshore islands reintegrated into Namibia.

Above: *The barren seaboard of the central Namib.*

Kayak Tours. Tours of varying duration are available and they offer kayakers the opportunity to view the seals and other marine species at close quarters.

Dune Sports

The dunes between Swakop-mund and Walvis Bay are ideally suited to a variety of dune sports, with paragliding and sand-boarding being the most popular. Although the dunes are relatively low when compared to those of Sossusvlei, sand-boarders can easily reach speeds of up to about 80kph (50mph). Guided quad-bike tours of the dunes, conducted from Swakopmund and Long Beach Resort, provide an adrenaline rush.

Dune Seven

Although not nearly as impressive as the sand dunes at Sossusvlei, **Dune Seven**, a few kilometres east of Walvis Bay along the Rooikop road, is the most easily accessible dune along this stretch of the coast. A scramble to the crest of the dune, approximately 50m (163ft) high, will not only make you aware of how tiring walking in the thick loose sand is but will also give you a bird's-eye view of the dune fields. Picnic facilities are available here for day visitors.

THE NAMIB-NAUKLUFT PARK

The Namib Desert has a surprising variety of landscape types. The section of the park between Lüderitz and the Kuiseb River is characterized by massive sand dunes, while the Namib section, between the Kuiseb and Swakop rivers, consists of vast quartzite gravel plains, bounded on the seaward side by a strip of dunes. Other components of the park include Sandwich, one of the most important coast wetlands in Africa, and the rugged Naukluft Mountains along the eastern edge of the desert.

Sandwich Harbour

In the early days of sail this lagoon, about 45km (30 miles) south of Walvis Bay, provided a safe anchorage to passing ships, hence it was called **Sandwich Harbour**. It has long since stopped serving this purpose, and is now a haven for a variety of birds.

Over the past 25 years the lagoon has been subject to dramatic natural changes. The reed-lined freshwater pools at its northern end have long since disappeared, while dynamic coastal processes have altered the nature of the coastline. What used to be a relatively easy drive to Sandwich should now be attempted only by experienced 4x4 drivers and only after obtaining local advice.

About 97% of the up to 238,000 waders, terns, cormorants, flamingoes and pelicans attracted to the wetlands of Sandwich Harbour are found on the mudflats to the south and the sandspit to the west of the lagoon. Both areas are, however, too far south for casual visits.

Sandwich Harbour is only accessible by four-wheel-drive, and vehicles are not allowed past the southern boundary of the angling area, so those who want to explore the lagoon will have to undertake a 1.5- to 2-hour walk from there. No overnight camping is allowed. Permits to visit Sandwich Harbour can be obtained from Namibia Wildlife Resorts in Swakopmund, or Windhoek.

DESERT DO'S AND DON'TS

The ecology of the Namib Desert is very fragile, and any unnecessary disturbance can cause irreparable damage. **Off-road driving** is especially cause for concern – tracks are unsightly and can scar the landscape for 50 years or more; the unique lichen fields of the Namib are destroyed; and the rare Damara tern, which breeds in the National West Coast Recreation Area, is threatened (see page 79). Always follow existing tracks.

Visitors must not collect any archaealogical artefacts, plants or plant material. Always carry a supply of wood with you when **camping** in the desert. Only use established camp sites, and always remove all your litter.

Below left: *Coastal birds in flight over the unspoilt Sandwich Harbour.* **Below:** *A curlew sandpiper.*

WELWITSCHIA

This botanical curiosity is restricted to the Namib Desert, from the Kuiseb River in the south to southwestern Angola. Although it has characteristics of both flowering and cone-bearing plants, it is classified as a Gymnosperm, an ancient plant order which includes cycads and conifers.

The tangled leaf-mass creates the impression that the plant has numerous leaves, but only two are produced. There are separate male and female plants; the female variety bear greenish-yellow cones banded with reddish brown that are larger than the salmon-coloured cones of the male. Average-sized specimens are between 500 and 600 years old, while the **Giant Welwitschia** is estimated to be about 2000 years old.

Namib Section **

Between the Kuiseb and Swakop rivers stretch sparsely vegetated gravel plains, occasionally interrupted by *inselbergen* (isolated remnant mountains).

In the shimmering midday heat mirages create visions of a massive lake on the horizon, a lone gemsbok takes on a grotesque shape and the plains seem totally devoid of life. Yet, the Namib is home to several fascinating animals and plants, all adapted to survive in the desert. Among the game to be seen here are herds of springbok, gemsbok, Hartmann's mountain zebra and bat-eared fox, as well as ostrich.

This section of the Namib-Naukluft Park is traversed by a network of well-maintained gravel roads which are negotiable by car (unless a signpost indicates otherwise). There are a number of picnic places for day visitors, as well as several delightful camp sites. However, facilities are limited to fireplaces and pit latrines.

Visitors may travel through the park on the proclaimed roads, but must obtain a permit to explore the signposted tourist roads (including the Welwitschia Drive) or to camp. Contact Namibia Wildlife Resorts in Windhoek or Swakopmund, weekdays.

One of the best ways to learn more about this fascinating area is to follow the 140km (87 miles) **Welwitschia Drive**. This self-guided interpretative route starts about 20km (12 miles) from Swakopmund and features the geology, lichens and some of

the interesting plants, including notable specimens of the *Welwitschia mirabilis*, of the Namib. The appropriately named **Moon Landscape** flanking the Swakop River Valley was formed over millions of years when the river's thousands of tributaries incised deeply into the soft deposits laid down about 450 million years ago.

Left: *The barren landscape of the Kuiseb Canyon.*
Opposite: *The strange welwitschia plant lives for more than 1000 years and produces just two leaves, which grow continuously, constantly splitting into ribbon-like strips.*

Kuiseb Canyon

Rising in the Khomas Hochland near Windhoek, the **Kuiseb River** has carved a spectacular canyon where it enters the Namib-Naukluft Park, about 165km (103 miles) from Swakopmund and about 230km (143 miles) from Windhoek. It is a wild landscape of badlands, crisscrossed by a maze of dry river courses which eventually make their way to the Kuiseb River.

The river is often dry for several years, but after heavy rains in the highlands it is transformed into a seething mass of water which rushes through a barren landscape. Floods wash away the sand that has been blown into the riverbed and thus the Kuiseb River plays an important role in preventing the sand dunes from encroaching onto the flat gravel plains that spread northward to the Swakop River. Subsequently, the river can flow for anything from a few days to over 100 days. The pools in the middle reaches supply water for gemsbok, Hartmann's mountain zebra, klipspringer and even the three troops of baboons which eke out an existence here.

About 9km (5.5 miles) west of the Kuiseb River camp site a signpost indicates the turnoff to **Carp Cliff**, overlooking the canyon far below. The view from here is spectacular in the late afternoon when the canyon walls take on a fiery orange hue in the last rays of the sun.

THE SHELTERING DESERT

A short walk from the viewpoint at **Carp Cliff** leads to a large overhang which has been immortalized in the classic book, *The Sheltering Desert*. During World War II two German geologists, Henno Martin and Herman Korn, who feared being interned, decided to flee into the desert rather than become involved in the war. Carp Cliff was the first of their three hideouts during the two-and-a-half years they spent in the Namib.

Their attempts at supplementing their meagre rations by hunting, collecting honey, fishing and growing vegetables in the Kuiseb river bed are related in the book, written by Henno Martin.

Below: *Ballooning over the southern Namib, not far from Sesriem in the Namib-Naukluft Park.*

Naukluft Mountains ★

Situated on the edge of the Namib, about 347km (216 miles) from Swakopmund and about 240km (149 miles) from Windhoek, the **Naukluft Mountains** form part of the dramatic escarpment which separates the coastal plain from the inland plateau. It is an extremely rugged mountain range, characterized by sheer cliffs, deeply incised river valleys and rolling hills.

The Naukluft complex was originally proclaimed as a sanctuary for the Hartmann's mountain zebra. Other large mammals found here include gemsbok, springbok, kudu, klipspringer and steenbok; the park also supports a healthy leopard population. To enable the gemsbok to migrate freely between the mountains and the dune sea further west, the complex is connected to the rest of the Namib-Naukluft Park by means of a narrow corridor.

Facilities here are limited to four camp sites with ablutions; advance reservations with Namibia Wildlife Resorts in Windhoek are essential. The rugged terrain is inaccessible to sedan cars, but there is a challenging two-day **4x4 trail** over 72km (45 miles). A secluded overnight camp provides accommodation at the end of the first day's drive. There are two **one-day hikes** for the more energetic, while the **Naukluft Hiking Trail** caters for the adventurous. The latter is a tough route with several options ranging from a four-day hike to a 120km (74.5 miles) eight-day circular route. The trail traverses difficult terrain and should not be attempted by inexperienced or unfit hikers or those who do not have a head for heights. On three sections of the trail, chains assist hikers up or down waterfalls. Two of the overnight huts along the trail are converted farmhouses that are equipped with bunks and mattresses, while basic stone shelters without any facilities (except

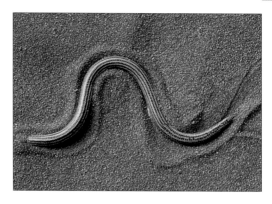

water) are provided at the six other overnight stops. Because of the heat in this part of the world, hiking is permitted only from 1 March to the third Friday in October and groups may consist of only 3–12 people. Contact Namibia Wildlife Resorts in Windhoek for reservations. This is a tough trail.

The Namib Dune Sea

South of the Kuiseb River is the Namib's vast **sea of dunes** ranging from the transverse dunes along the coast to the star dunes near the eastern edge of the desert.

Among the fascinating **animals** which are endemic to the Namib are the side-winding adder, the almost translucent web-footed gecko, the Namib golden mole and a host of *toktokkie*, or tenebrionid, beetles. To survive in this inhospitable environment where temperatures soar over 40°C (104°F), these desert creatures have adapted in several ways. They live underground where temperature fluctuations are minimal, or climb onto plants to escape from the hot surface of the sand. Fundamental to their survival are the dense banks of fog which supplement the meagre rainfall, and the desert-adapted beetles collect the precipitation from the fog in a variety of ways. Some beetle species dig shallow trenches to trap the fog, while others obtain their water by doing a headstand, facing the fog-laden wind, so that water droplets trickle down into their mouths.

Another key to the survival of the smaller desert animals is detritus, which consists of windblown plant material, dead insects and animal droppings. Detritus forms the basis of the food of the detritivores, like the tenebrionid beetle, which in turn provide a source of food for a host of carnivores, like Anchieta's dune lizard, which in turn is preyed on by the side-winding adder.

Above: *Desert reptiles include the Fitzsimmons' burrowing skink.*

MOUNTAIN ZEBRA

The **Hartmann's mountain zebra** is closely related to the Cape mountain zebra, which occurs much further south in the Cape Midlands and the mountains separating the Little and Great Karoo. The range of the Hartmann's mountain zebra extends from the Orange River northward along the escarpment into south-western Angola and eastwards into the Khomas Hochland in central Namibia and the western part of the Etosha National Park. One of the major differences between the two mountain zebras is that the dark and light stripes of Hartmann's are more or less equally wide, while the dark stripes of the Cape mountain zebra are much wider than the lighter stripes. The former is also slightly taller than the southern subspecies.

Above: *The Sesriem camp site at sunrise.*

Sesriem and Sossusvlei ★★★

A visit to Sesriem, the gateway to Sossusvlei, one of Namibia's prime tourist attractions, is well worth the drive of 350km (218 miles) from Swakopmund, or 330km (205 miles) from Windhoek. Facilities at **Sesriem** at the edge of the dunes, are limited to camp sites shaded by camel thorn trees, ablutions, a shop, filling station and swimming pool. Contact Namibia Wildlife Resorts in Windhoek for reservations.

The **Sossusvlei Lodge** adjacent to Sesriem offers accommodation in canvas- and adobe-walled double-bed units. In addition the lodge has a restaurant, alfresco dining terrace, bar and swimming pool.

Some 4km (2.5 miles) south of Sesriem the **Tsauchab River** has carved a deep, narrow canyon through the conglomerates and after good rains the pools in the canyon retain their water for several months. Sesriem means 'six thongs' in Afrikaans and the name refers to the way the early pioneers in the region drew water from the pools by lowering a bucket tied to the end of six ox-thongs.

From Sesriem a tar road follows the Tsauchab valley past the much-photographed Dune 45 to reach the 2x4 parking area after 60km (37 miles). The last 5km (3 miles) of the road to **Sossusvlei** is through heavy sand, suitable only for a four-wheel-drive. The vlei, a greyish-white clay pan which is virtually surrounded by towering orange sand dunes, is often dry for several years, but after good rains the Tsauchab River sometimes floods the vlei.

Though the dunes are impressive – they measure up to 325m (1066ft) – it should be borne in mind that they are not freestanding as they rest on a sandstone terrace.

An early start is advisable as the colour transformation of the dunes is at its best immediately after sunrise. Also, early mornings are the best time to attempt to scale one of the dunes in the vicinity of Sossusvlei (a daunting undertaking!). A few picnic sites under tall camel thorn trees are available at the vlei, as well as toilets.

Upmarket accommodation near the park is available at **Sossusvlei Wilderness Camp**. The stone, timber and thatch chalets are built among the boulders of a rocky outcrop with breathtaking views over the surrounding plains.

NamibRand Nature Reserve

Covering some 200,000ha (494,200 acres) of plains, magnificent dunes, granite outcrops and mountains, this reserve lies 26km (16 miles) south of Sesriem as the crow flies. To the west, it borders on the Namib-Naukluft Park for over 120km (75 miles), while the Nubib Mountains lie to the east. Home to herds of gemsbok, springbok, zebra and a host of smaller creatures, the reserve's main attractions are its awe-inspiring scenery and solitude. Activities include scenic drives and guided walks. Balloon safaris start from Camp Mwisho, while tailor-made overnight walking safaris are conducted by Toktokkie Trails.

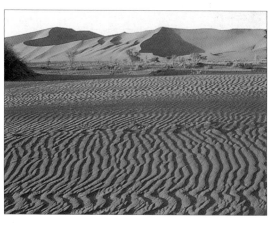

Below: *Neatly corrugated landscape at Sossusvlei.*

The Namib at a Glance

The temperate months of **October** to **March** best time to visit **coast**, but occasional hot, dry easterly winds. Cooler months from **May** to **September** best time to visit **Namib**, but strong easterly winds bring high temperatures.

Air Namibia operates several scheduled weekly flights between Walvis Bay and Windhoek, tel: (061) 2996444. Small **air charters** operate from Swakopmund and Walvis Bay. TransNamib operates six overnight passenger **train** services between Windhoek and Walvis Bay a week, tel: (061) 2982032. Intercape Mainliner offers **coach service** between Windhoek and Walvis Bay several times a week, tel: (061) 227847.
Swakopmund is 350km (217 miles) from Windhoek along a **tarred road**. **Gravel-surface roads** between Lüderitz or Maltahöhe and Walvis Bay or Swakopmund are generally in quite a good condition.

Most of the popular tourist attractions in the Namib are accessible by car along **gravel-surface roads**, generally in good condition. However, unless you are with an organized tour or safari, make sure you have basic spares, water and a second spare wheel as some of the back roads in this remote area carry very little traffic.
Car hire in Swakopmund – Avis, tel: (064) 402527; Budget, tel: (064) 463380; Europcar, tel: (064) 400383; Hertz, tel: (064) 461826; Imperial, tel: (064) 207391. In Walvis Bay – Avis, tel: (064) 209633; Budget, tel: (064) 204128; Europcar, tel: (064) 203651, Imperial, tel: (064) 207391.

Swakopmund
Hansa Hotel: tel: (064) 414200, fax 414299.
Hotel Europahof: tel: (064) 405061, fax: 402391.
Beach Lodge: tel: (064) 400933, fax: 400934.
Strand Hotel: tel: (064) 400315, fax: 404942.
Swakopmund Hotel and Entertainment Centre: tel: (064) 4105200, fax: 415360.

Namib-Naukluft Park Area
Ababis, at foot of Naukluft Mountains: near several well-known attractions in the Namib Desert, tel: (063) 683080.
Büllsport Guest Farm, at foot of Naukluft Mountains: walking trails, horse riding, four-wheel-drive trips to nearby attractions, tel: (063) 693371.
Sossusvlei Lodge, adjacent to Sesriem, tel: (+2721 9304564), fax: (061) 255488.
Namib-Naukluft Lodge, bordering Namib-Naukluft Park: trips to Sossusvlei, tel: (061) 372100.
Sossusvlei Mountain Lodge, in

NamibRand Nature Reserve: exclusive accommodation, tel: (27 11) 8094300, fax: 8094400.
Sossusvlei Wilderness Camp, close to Sossusvlei: luxury accommodation, ballooning, trips to Sossusvlei, tel: (061) 274500, fax: (+2721) 9304574.
Weltevrede Rest Camp, at the foot of the Naukluft Mountains: close to Sossusvlei, typical Namibian hospitality, tel: (063) 683073, fax: 683074.
NamibRand Nature Reserve, adjoining Namib-Naukluft Park: three accomodation options, tel: (061) 230616, fax: 220102.

Walvis Bay
Lagoon Lodge, 2 Kovambo Nujoma Drive: tel: (064) 200850, fax: 200851.
Langholm Hotel Garni, 24 2nd Street West: tel: (064) 209230, fax: 209430.
Walvis Bay Protea Hotel, cnr Sam Nujoma Avenue and 10th Rd: tel: (064) 209560, fax: 209565.

Swakopmund
Café Anton, Bismarck Street: for tea, coffee and light meals, tel: (064) 400331.
Erich's, Daniël Tjongarero Street: for seafood (fresh line-fish, rock lobster and oysters): tel: (064) 405141.
Kucki's Pub, Tobias Haiyenko Street: a popular pub with an informal, busy atmosphere and some really excellent food, tel: (064) 402407.
Platform One Restaurant,

The Namib at a Glance

Swakopmund Hotel and Entertainment Centre: excellent buffet and à la carte restaurant, tel: (064) 4105200.
Putensen Bakery and Café, Sam Nujoma Avenue: for tea, coffee and light snacks, tel: (064) 402034.
The Tug, The Jetty: a bar in an authentic tug: excellent seafood and ocean views, tel: (064) 402356.
Western Saloon, Tobias Haiyenko Street: small, but offers personalized service; renowned for seafood and steaks, tel: (064) 405395.

Walvis Bay
The Raft Restaurant, Esplanade: good food and excellent views over Walvis Bay lagoon, tel: (064) 204877.

TOURS AND EXCURSIONS

For half- and full-day tours of **Swakopmund**, **Walvis Bay, Namib Desert**, **Sandwich Lagoon** and **Cape Cross** contact Charly's Desert Tours, tel: (064) 404341; Swakop Tour Company, tel: (064) 404088.
Scenic **Balloon flights** are operated from Camp Mwisho and from the Sesriem area by Namib Sky Adventure Safaris, tel: (063) 293233, fax: 293241.
For **angling trips**, from rock-surf to deep-sea fishing, contact Sunrise Tours, tel: (064) 404561 (in Swakopmund). For **dolphin and seal cruises**, contact Mola Mola

Safaris in Walvis Bay, tel: (064) 205511.
Flights over areas along the coast that are inaccessible by vehicle, as well as over the Namib Desert, including Sossusvlei and further afield, offered by Pleasure Flights, Sam Nujoma Avenue, Swakopmund, tel and fax: (064) 404500, and in Walvis Bay by Bay Air, 242 11th Street, tel: (064) 204319.
For **sea kayak trips** on Walvis Bay Lagoon contact Jeanne Meintjies in Walvis Bay, tel and fax: (064) 203144.
Camel Farm, tel: (064) 400363.

USEFUL TELEPHONE NUMBERS

Namibia Wildlife Resorts, Woermann House, Am Ankerplatz, Swakopmund, tel: (064) 402172.
Namibia Wildlife Resorts, Windhoek, tel: (061) 236975 for reservations and information, fax: 224900.
Namib I information office, Sam Nujoma Avenue, Swakopmund,

tel: (064) 404827.
Shops and galleries (Swakopmund): African Art Jewellers, Hansa Hotel Building, Hendrik Witbooi Street, tel: (064) 405566; African Kirikara Art, Am Ankerplatz, tel: (064) 463146; Casa Anin, The Arcade, tel: (064) 405 910; Die Muschel, Hendrik Witbooi Street, tel: (064) 402874; Stonetique, 27 Albertina Amathila Avenue, tel: (064) 405403; Hobby Horse, Brauhaus Arcade, Hendrik Witbooi Street, tel: (064) 402875; Engelhard Design, 55 Sam Nujoma Avenue, tel: (064) 404606; Karakulia, Rakotoka Street, tel: (064) 461415; Namib Stamps, Commercial Bank Arcade, Sam Nujoma Avenue, tel: (064) 405560; Peter's Antiques, 24 Tobias Hainyeko Street, tel: (064) 405624; Swakopmund Tannery, Leutwein Street, tel: (064) 402633.
Swakopmund Museum, Strand Street, tel: (064) 402046.

WALVIS BAY	J	F	M	A	M	J	J	A	S	O	N	D
AVERAGE TEMP. °F	63	64	63	60	60	59	55	55	55	57	60	63
AVERAGE TEMP. °C	17	18	17	16	16	15	13	13	13	14	15	17
HOURS OF SUN DAILY	7	6	7	7	8	8	8	7	6	7	7	7
SEA TEMP. °F	68	66	64	63	63	59	59	59	59	59	61	61
SEA TEMP. °C	20	19	18	17	17	15	15	15	15	15	16	16
RAINFALL in	0	0	0	0	0	0	0	0	0	0	0	0
RAINFALL mm	1	1	7	1	0	3	0	0	0	0	0	0
DAYS OF RAINFALL	1	1	1	1	0	1	0	0	1	0	1	0
DAYS OF MIST/FOG	8	8	11	16	16	12	15	15	12	9	9	8

5
Skeleton Coast
and Kaokoveld

Situated in the remote northwestern corner of Namibia, the **Skeleton Coast** and the adjoining Kaokoveld are among the most scenic areas of southern Africa. The barren, windswept coast is often shrouded in mist for days on end, and early mariners feared this area which earned itself the reputation of being the world's largest shipping graveyard. It is a world of intricately patterned sand dunes, shimmering saltpans and plains stretching into the distance, and the habitat of a fascinating variety of animals and plants.

Adjoining the Skeleton Coast is **Kaokoland**, a region renowned for its rugged scenery and one of the world's last wilderness areas. It is the home of the Himba and a sanctuary to desert-dwelling elephant and black rhino.

South of Kaokoland lies **Damaraland**, a land of stark contrasts ranging from high mountains to rolling grasslands and plains littered with rock. This inhospitable region has many rewards for those who are prepared to tolerate excessive temperatures and bumpy roads. Not only is the **Brandberg** Namibia's highest mountain, but it is also rich in rock paintings, including the renowned White Lady. Another open-air art gallery can be viewed at **Twyfelfontein,** which is considered to be one of the largest collections of rock engravings in Africa.

The **National West Coast Recreation Area**, a 200km (124 miles) stretch of coast north of Swakopmund, is an angler's paradise, attracting fishermen from afar. Here some of the most extensive lichen fields in the world are found, and the rare Damara tern has its breeding nests.

CLIMATE

The **coast** is often blanketed in **fog**, mostly in winter. Summers are sunny, although the annual average temperature is only 16°C (61°F). Rain is rare, with a mean of about 16mm (0.6in) a year.

Summer highs of up to 40°C (104°F) are recorded in the **Kaokoveld**. Winter days are warm, but evenings are chilly and the east **wind** brings higher temperatures. The annual summer rainfall is erratic, usually less than 100mm (4in).

Opposite: *Kaokoland, is one of the last remaining wilderness areas in Southern Africa.*

DON'T MISS

*** **Skeleton Coast concession area:** visit this restricted
area by joining an exclusive
fly-in safari.
*** **Twyfelfontein:** admire the
renowned open-air gallery of
rock engravings.
** **Uniab Delta Walk:**
discover the unique beauty of
the Skeleton Coast on foot.
** **Cape Cross Seal Reserve:**
get close-up views of thousands of seals at this accessible
breeding colony.
** **Kaokoland:** explore one of
the last wilderness areas in a
four-wheel-drive.

NATIONAL WEST COAST RECREATION AREA

This 200km (124 miles) stretch of the Namib coast between the Swakop and Ugab rivers is one of the most popular **angling areas** – indeed, the prime angling destination – in southern Africa, and it attracts thousands of fishing enthusiasts each year.

Galjoen, a species favouring gullies, reefs and rocky areas, is one of the most popular light-tackle fish, and there is a limit of eight per bona fide angler. Other popular angling species include kob, or kabeljou, white steenbras and blacktail. To ensure that Namibia's rock and surf species are not over-exploited, angling regulations are strictly enforced and fishermen must ensure that they are familiar with them. Contact the Ministry of Fisheries and Marine Resources for more information.

There are several campsites along the coast, most of them named rather unimaginatively after their distance in miles from Swakopmund. However, except for **Mile Four** just outside the town (which has bungalows, caravan and camping sites, ablution facilities and communal kitchens, freezers and a laundry), camping facilities are all quite basic and are used mainly by fishermen. For reservations and information contact Namibia Wildlife Resorts in Windhoek.

The small fishing settlement of **Wlotzkas Baken** is about 30km (18.5 miles) north of Swakopmund. However, the houses here are all privately owned, and the village has no tourist facilities at all.

Henties Bay, the only town along this stretch of

Left: *The Cape Cross Seal Reserve is home to thousands of these marine mammals, and to great numbers of Cape cormorants.*

coast, is about 75km (47 miles) north of Swakopmund. From its humble beginnings of a few fishermen's shacks in the 1930s it has expanded into one of Namibia's prime holiday resorts. Facilities in the town include a hotel, several shops and filling stations and a rather novel 9-hole golf course which has grass greens but sand fairways.

Cape Cross Seal Reserve **
The **Cape Cross Seal Reserve**, about 120km (74.5 miles) north of Swakopmund, is one of 16 breeding colonies of the Cape fur seal along the Namibian coast.

Nearly 75% of Namibia's estimated 700,000 Cape fur seals can be found south of Hollam's Bird Island, which is about 200km (124 miles) south of Walvis Bay. At Cape Cross the seal population fluctuates between an estimated 80,000 and 260,000.

The sanctuary is open to the public daily from 10:00 to 17:00. With permit in hand (obtainable from the office at the reserve), you can observe the seals at close quarters from behind a wall.

Also of interest here is an authentic replica of the stone cross or *padrão* erected by Diego Cão, the first European to set foot on Namibian soil, in 1486. To the left of the *padrão* is a granite replica which was put here on the orders of Kaiser Wilhelm after the original was removed to Germany in 1893.

A FRAGILE ECOLOGY

Off-road driving in the Namib poses a threat to the **lichen fields** – the most extensive in the world – and the **Damara tern**, a visitor from West Africa that arrives in September and October to breed along the coast. The birds are small, grey and white, and have a black cap, make their nests up to 5km (3 miles) inland on the gravel plains and between the dunes, and lay one egg. The coast of the Namib is the summer home of up to 14,000 of these rare birds. The Namib's wide variety of more than 100 fascinating species of lichen ranges from the wind-blown types resembling bits of dead plant material to the orange tufts of the *Teloschistes*. The key to the survival of these colourful and intriguing plants is the fog which blankets the coast for more than 100 days a year.

DAMARALAND

Adjacent to the National West Coast Recreation Area lies Damaraland with its majestic flat-topped mountains, spectacular gorges, wide open plains and art treasures inherited from the earlier inhabitants.

Spitzkoppe

This imposing granite rock formation is a familiar land-mark north of the road between Usakos (51km/32 miles away) and Swakopmund (180km/112 miles away). Towering some 700m (2296ft) above the surrounding plains, the sharply pointed *inselberg* is known as the **Groot Spitzkoppe**. From a distance the dome-shaped granite outcrops flanking the Groot (or large) Spitzkoppe resemble traditional African huts, hence the Afrikaans name *Pondok* (meaning grass hut). Just 15km (9 miles) to the west are the Klein (or small) Spitzkoppe.

A chain at the eastern end of the Pondok Mountains helps visitors to scramble up the steep rock to **Bushman's Paradise** – a small basin tucked away between the domes. Compared to the sparsely vegetated surrounding plains, this amphitheatre is indeed a paradise and the rock art in the overhang is testimony to the people who

Below: *The sunset grandeur of Spitzkoppe, inland from the Skeleton Coast. The region of Damaraland is renowned for its San rock art.*

once sheltered here. The paintings have been vandalized, but the overhang is still worth a visit.

There are a number of campsites, sheltered by massive boulders, around the base of the Spitzkoppe; traditional Damara huts can also be hired on a first come, first served basis. Fireplaces, refuse bins and basic ablution facilities are provided.

Above: *Namibia's diverse regions support a variety of reptiles. The rock monitor, or leguaan, has a powerful muscular tail that it uses for self-defence.*

Brandberg

The steep slopes of this forbidding mountain, located about 170km (106 miles) west of Omaruru, are littered with gigantic granite boulders which are transformed into a glowing reddish-orange colour in the rays of the setting sun. This, combined with the dark basalt at the base, gave rise to its descriptive name, **Brandberg**, which means 'burning mountain'.

It has one of the richest collections of rock paintings in the world (more than 43,000), best known of which is the famous **White Lady** frieze. The painting was executed in an overhang in the Tsisab Ravine on the northeastern side of the mountain and was 'discovered' in 1917.

The **Brandberg (Daureb) mountain guides** offer guided walks to the White Lady frieze as well as other nearby rock painting sites, and will also provide an insight into the flora and fauna of the mountain. They are based at the Tsisab Ravine parking area. Owing to the midday heat, walks are best undertaken early in the morning and you should allow about four hours there and back. Carry at least two litres (about four pints) of water and wear a sun hat and comfortable footwear.

Bungalows, a restaurant and shady campsites are available at the nearby Brandberg White Lady Lodge.

THE WHITE LADY

The 'White Lady Procession' was discovered in 1917, but attracted worldwide attention only after several works were published in the late 1950s by the French prehistorian, the Abbé Henri Breuil. He immediately 'identified' the central figure as a white female with Mediterranean features. Subsequently, however, the race and sex of the figure were increasingly questioned and it is now generally accepted that the White Lady is neither white, nor female. The figure displays the physical characteristics of a male carrying a bow and arrow, while the pale colour is now believed to represent body paint.

The Brandberg is Namibia's highest mountain, and the peak **Königstein**, at 2579m (8461ft) the highest point in the country, is a formidable challenge. The rugged terrain, scarcity of water and very high temperatures restrict this demanding expedition to fit and experienced hikers only. At least four days are required for a return trip to Namibia's highest peak.

Khorixas

Although the administrative centre of the Kunene region, Khorixas is a rather uninspiring, dusty town with little to offer the tourist. However, there are many attractions in the vicinity worth exploring and the **Khorixas rest camp** on the outskirts serves as a convenient base.

Set aside a morning to visit Twyfelfontein, the Petrified Forest, and the Burnt Mountain. Make an early start because of the hot temperatures at midday.

Petrified Forest

The turnoff to the **Petrified Forest** is signposted about 43km (27 miles) west of the town. These trees were uprooted elsewhere some 200 million years ago and were

Below: *Damaraland scene. This region is mostly rugged, sometimes gentle, always beautiful.*

Left: *Some of the 2400 or more petroglyphs, or rock engravings, on view among the jumbled out-crops and boulders of the Twyfelfontein (meaning doubtful spring) area. Some of them date back about 5000 years.*

swept along by rivers in flood, covered by sediments and subsequently uncovered by erosion. Local community guides provide an insight into the area and also ensure that pieces of petrified wood are not removed. Facilities for tourists include a large picnic area (under thatch), toilets and covered parking.

Twyfelfontein ★★★

Just before Twyfelfontein is the **AbaHuab campsite**, a convenient base for visitors who are geared for camping. **Twyfelfontein** is just a few kilometres away from the campsite, and a small entrance fee is charged. Here visitors have the opportunity to view one of the largest collections of rock engravings in Africa. The engravings were chiselled painstakingly into the rock slabs littering the slopes of a low, flat-topped mountain, and one cannot help but marvel at how realistic and well proportioned they are.

Two well-defined **circular walks** have been laid out here. Highlights of the short option, which takes about an hour to complete, include the famous Twyfelfontein elephant, a rhinoceros with spoor instead of feet and the much-photographed lion panel. The longer route takes about 90 minutes and you will no doubt be intrigued by the 'Dancing Kudu', which is surrounded by numerous geometric patterns. Other points of interest along this

---

TWYFELFONTEIN ROCK ENGRAVINGS

Unidentified antelope represent a quarter of the 2400 engravings recorded at Twyfelfontein, while gemsbok and springbok head the list of identifiable antelope with 67 and 34 engravings respectively. The other most commonly depicted identifiable animals are: giraffe (316), ostrich (283), zebra (175) and rhinoceros (144). In addition, 383 animal spoor are also portrayed. Nearly 15% of the engravings represent abstract patterns or relate to humans (in the form of footprints, handprints and so on).

route are the remains of huts built by pre-colonial herders and some of the relatively few rock paintings found at Twyfelfontein. To ensure the preservation of the rock engravings you must be accompanied by a guide, based at the parking area. Comfortable walking shoes are essential and remember to carry sufficient water. Early mornings and late afternoons are the best times to view the engravings. **Twyfelfontein Country Lodge** and **Mowani Mountain Camp** are both close to Twyfelfontein.

Organ Pipes and Burnt Mountain

Two other well-known geological features close to Twyfelfontein are the Organ Pipes and the Burnt Mountain. The **Organ Pipes**, a distinctive series of dolerite pillars that have been exposed by erosion, can be seen in the small gorge on the left-hand side of the road leading to the **Burnt Mountain**. The flat-topped mountain derives its name from the piles of blackened limestone at its base; the chunks of black dolerite combined with the crudely shaped rocks in an amazing variety of colours create the impression that the mountain has been burnt by a fierce fire. Early morning and late afternoon are the best times to visit the mountain as the kaleidescope of colours is most impressive then.

Vingerklip (Finger Rock)

Although slightly off the beaten track, a visit to the **Vingerklip**, 75km (47 miles) east of Khorixas, is well worth the detour. The 35m (115ft) column of limestone conglomerate and the surrounding table-top mountains are relics of an earlier plateau which was subsequently eroded by the Ugab River. The formation overlooks the nearby **Vingerklip Lodge** which offers luxury accommodation.

Palmwag Lodge

The rustic reed-and-thatch **Palmwag Lodge** is an ideal base from which to explore the more remote regions of northern Damaraland. It overlooks a spring where desert-dwelling elephants sometimes quench their thirst and takes its name from the makalani palms that grow around the reed-lined spring. Facilities offered at the lodge include a small shop, a restaurant, swimming pools and a campsite.

Palmwag is at the centre of the area inhabited by the world-renowned desert-dwelling elephants and black rhino, and the possibility of seeing these rare animals is one of the main attractions of the area. However, gemsbok, springbok and giraffe are more commonly sighted.

The lodge is accessible by car, but you will need a four-wheel-drive vehicle to explore the surrounding countryside. Access is strictly controlled and do-it-yourself visitors must obtain a permit at Palmwag before venturing into the concession area. Alternatively, you can join one of the safaris offered by Palmwag Lodge and Travel Shop.

Etendeka Mountain Camp

The tented camp in the adjacent **Etendeka concession area** lies among rugged mountains. Although several species of game, including desert-dwelling elephant and black rhino, make seasonal visits to the area, the emphasis here is on the fascinating plantlife and smaller creatures, like lizards, spiders and ants, which are often overlooked. The camp is accessible by four-wheel-drive vehicle only, so guests are met at the nearby airstrip or at the veterinary fence.

DESERT ELEPHANTS

The desert-dwelling elephants of Damaraland and Kaokoland are not a distinct species or subspecies, but they are unique. They can go without water for up to four days; during times of drought they walk up to 60km (37 miles) from their feeding grounds to reach waterholes. Unlike other elephants, they are careful in utilizing their food resources. The key to their survival is their intimate knowledge of the harsh desert. Only a small population of the estimated 600 elephants in northwestern Namibia are found between the Hoanib and Hoarusib rivers and can be classified as truly desert-dwelling.

Opposite: *The remarkable Vingerklip (Finger Rock).*
Below: *Desert-adapted elephants in Kaokoland.*

Khowarib Schlucht

The **Khowarib Schlucht Community Tourist Camp**, 76km (46 miles) north of Palmwag, on the banks of the Hoanib River, is an oasis in this arid region as here water from a spring flows in the otherwise dry river. Accommodation ranges from campsites on the river-bank to traditional Damara and Himba huts on the high terrace overlooking the Hoanib. The camp is one of several tourism ventures in Damaraland initiated to enable the local people to share in the benefits of tourism. Visitors must be completely self-sufficient.

Warmquelle, Ongongo and Sesfontein

The small settlement of **Warmquelle**, 17km (11 miles) east of Sesfontein, is named after the lukewarm thermal spring, surrounded by shade-giving trees, that rises here. Nearby the **Ongongo Falls**, which cascades into a crystal-clear pool, invites the hot and weary traveller to cool off after a hot day's drive through the Kaokoveld. Basic campsites as well as picnic facilities for day visitors are available. At **Sesfontein**, which takes its name from the springs surfacing here, visitors can overnight in the historic Fort Sesfontein which has been beautifully restored, with restaurant, swimming pool and campsites.

Hobatere Lodge

Bordering Etosha, Damaraland and Kaokoland, and 80km (50 miles) from Kamanjab, **Hobatere Lodge** is an ideal stopover for the visitor on a safari into Kaokoland. The 35,000ha (86,487 acres) Hobatere Game Park is a sanctuary to a wide variety of game including lion, elephant, springbok and Hartmann's mountain zebra, as well as about 177 bird species. Accommodation at the lodge, which is surrounded by spectacular granite hills, is provided in comfortable thatched rondavels with en suite facilities. The lodge also has a restaurant, an open-air *boma*, swimming pool and campsites. Game and night drives, as well as guided walks, are conducted.

HISTORY OF SESFONTEIN

Sesfontein derives its name from the Nama word *nanious*, which means 'six fountains'. Following the outbreak of cattle plague in 1896, a post was established here by the German colonial administration in order to control the movement of livestock. Later, the post was used to control poaching and the smuggling of firearms and ammunition to Angola.

A military station was built at Sesfontein in 1902, and in 1905–6 the building was converted to a fort. The military post was closed in 1909, but three police officers were stationed here until the police station was closed five years later.

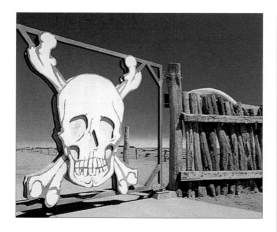

SKELETON COAST PARK

Covering approximately 1,600,000ha (3,953,683 acres), the **Skeleton Coast Park** stretches from the Ugab River northward along the coast to the Kunene River and about 40km (25 miles) inland. It is a solitary landscape of gravel plains, sand dunes and canyons. The southern zone is accessible to tourists, while the northern zone is managed as a wilderness area.

Southern Section ★★

The southern section of the park is accessible along the coastal road via the Ugab River gate in the south or through the Springbokwasser gate in the west. It is an angler's paradise that attracts thousands of hopeful fishermen every year. The most popular catches are galjoen and kabeljou, while white steenbras and sea barbel are also caught.

The campsite at **Torra Bay** is closed for 10 months of the year, but in the summer months of December and January it is packed with angling enthusiasts. At **Terrace Bay**, formerly a mining settlement, accommodation is inclusive of three meals a day, but the bungalows are somewhat spartan and lack atmosphere. Contact Namibia Wildlife Resorts in Windhoek for reservations and information.

Above: *The forbidding entrance to the Skeleton Coast park at Ugab.*

Right: *The bone-dry bed of the Ugab River, venue for a challenging hiking trail.*

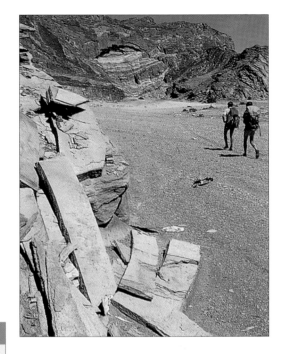

For those who would like to explore some of the scenic attractions on foot there is the **Uniab Delta Walk**, which takes two to three hours to complete. One of the highlights of the route is a spectacular waterfall which plunges into a narrow pink gorge.

Another option for the energetic is the three-day **Ugab Hiking Trail,** conducted in the Ugab River valley, on the second and fourth Thursday of every month from April to October. The hike alternates between windswept plains and the rugged river valley with its spectacular folded layers of schist, dolomite and marble. Groups are guided by a conservation official who will point out the interesting facets of the area. Hikers should be fit as they must carry all their equipment and food; nights are spent camping under the stars. Contact Namibia Wildlife Resorts in Windhoek for reservations and information.

Northern Section ★★★

The northern sector of the park between the Hoanib and the Kunene rivers covers 800,000ha (1,976,841 acres) and is managed as a wilderness area. Because of the very fragile ecology and isolation of the region, access is restricted to a concession area between the Hoarusib and Nadas rivers; visitors can explore this part of the park only by joining a **fly-in** safari operated by Wilderness Safaris Namibia.

KAOKOLAND

East of the Skeleton Coast Park lies a very rugged area that is nevertheless one of Namibia's most scenic regions – **Kaokoland**. It is a starkly beautiful landscape of table-top mountains, cone-shaped hills and rock-strewn plains where desert-dwelling elephant, rhino and giraffe roam. The region is also the home of the nomadic Himba, who migrate seasonally with their herds of livestock in search of grazing, much as they did a century ago.

Covering some 49,500km² (19,112 sq miles), Kaokoland stretches from the Hoanib River northward to the Kunene. Among its scenic attractions are the **Kunene River** with the renowned **Epupa** and **Ruacana** falls, as well as the rapids at **Enyandi** and **Ondorusu**. Other interesting features of the landscape include **Marienfluss**, an extensive plain over 50km (31 miles) long, and the adjacent **Hartmann Valley**, as well as the rugged **Otjihipa**, **Baynes** and **Zebra** mountains.

The roads in this large, sparsely populated area are no more than tracks, negotiable by four-wheel-drive

Left: *Himba women, Kaokoland.*

Right: *The perennial Kunene River's spectacular Epupa Falls in northern Kaokoland. The remote Kunene area is scenically beautiful and still untamed (although poaching reduced the numbers of wild animals in the region in the early 1980s). Attention is being paid to future development for tourism here, and canoe trips down the river are now offered.*

EPUPA AND RUACANA FALLS

The **Epupa Falls**, about 190km (118 miles) upstream of the Kunene River mouth, is one of Kaokoland's most breathtaking sights. Here the river fans out into a number of channels before cascading into a deep gorge. There are plans to build Namibia's second hydro-electric scheme downstream of Epupa, but no agreement on the location has been reached.

The well-known **Ruacana Falls**, about 120km (74.5 miles) upstream, is dry for most of the year, but after good rains the Kunene becomes a seething, thundering mass of water that tumbles into the 120m (394ft) deep gorge.

---

vehicles only. Always travel in a party of at least two vehicles to safeguard against being stranded in the event of a breakdown as it could take several days before another vehicle passes in this remote area. To get the most out of a visit to Kaokoland, you should plan to spend at least five days in the region, and make sure that you are well equipped and prepared (firewood, fresh water, ample fuel supplies, a mosquito net and anti-malaria medication are essential).

Opuwo, the administrative centre of the area, is a frontier town in the true sense of the word. It does not have any tourist attractions, but is the only settlement in the region where fuel and a limited supply of groceries can be purchased.

Several tour operators offer guided safaris into Kaokoland; if you are unfamiliar with the area, your best option is to join one of these.

Skeleton Coast and Kaokoveld at a Glance

Along the **coast**, moderate temperatures but windy and misty year-round. Rain is rare. **November** to **March** best for angling. **Inland**, cooler months **May** to **August** best. High temperatures and flash floods in summer. Most rain between January and March.

Air Namibia, tel: (061) 2996444, fax: 2996168, has several scheduled weekly flights from Windhoek to Walvis Bay. **Landing strips** at Henties Bay, Mile 108, Torra Bay and Terrace Bay, and near Palmwag, Etendeka, Hobatere and Epupa; contact (Windhoek) Desert Air, tel: (061) 228101, fax: 248316; Comav, tel: (061) 227512, fax: 245612; Westair, tel: (061) 221091, fax: 232778; (Swakopmund) Pleasure Flights, tel and fax: (064) 404500.

Roads on Skeleton Coast accessible by car; four-wheel-drive needed to go off the beaten track for angling. **Car** and **four-wheel-drive hire** in Swakopmund (see page 74). **Khorixas** accessible by tarred road via Outjo. Attractions in **Damaraland** reached by gravel-surface roads, accessible by car but conditions vary. Party of at least two four-wheel-drives essential in **Kaokoland** as roads not sign-posted and often mere tracks.

National West Coast Recreation Area
Mile 4 camp site: tel: (064) 461781.
Hotel De Duine, Henties Bay: tel: (064) 500001.
Cape Cross Lodge at Cape Cross: Luxury rooms, tel: (064) 694012, fax: 694013.

Kaokoland
Kunene River Lodge, tel: (065) 274300, fax: 274301.

Damaraland
Etendeka Mountain Camp: tel: (061) 226979, fax: 226999.
Hobatere Lodge, Kamanjab: tel: (067) 330261, fax: 330268.
Damaraland Camp: tel: (061) 274500.
Mowani Mountain Camp: tel: (061) 232009, fax: 222574.
Palmwag Lodge: tel: (064) 404459, fax 404664.
Twyfelfontein Country Lodge: tel: (061) 374750, fax: 256598.

National West Coast Recreation Area
Spitzkoppe Restaurant, Henties Bay: seafood and steaks, tel: (064) 500394.
De Duine Hotel Restaurant, Henties Bay, tel: (064) 500001.

Damaraland
Restaurants at **Khorixas**, **Palmwag** and **Fort Sesfontein**.

Palmwag Lodge and Travel Shop offers **tours** of **Damaraland** from camps situated at Palmwag and on the Kunene River, tel: (064) 404459, fax: 404664. Kaokohimba Safaris specializes in overland and fly-in **safaris** to **Damaraland, Kaokoland** and the Kunene River, tel/fax: (061) 222378. Contact Wilderness Safaris Namibia to arrange **fly-in safaris** to the concession area in the Skeleton Coast Park, tel: (061) 274500, fax: 239455. For **canoeing** on the **Kunene River**, contact Felix Unite, tel: (2721) 6701300, fax: 6701400.

Ministry of Fisheries and Marine Resources, tel: (064) 405744.
Namibia Wildlife Resorts, Swakopmund, tel: (064) 402172.

SKELETON COAST	J	F	M	A	M	J	J	A	S	O	N	D
AVERAGE TEMP. °F	66	66	66	63	61	59	57	55	57	59	61	64
AVERAGE TEMP. °C	19	19	19	17	16	15	14	13	14	15	16	18
HOURS OF SUN DAILY	6	7	7	5	4	4	3	4	3	5	7	7
RAINFALL in	0	0	0.5	0	0	0	0	0	0	0	0	0
RAINFALL mm	3	3	0	1	0	0	0	0	0	0	0	0
DAYS OF RAINFALL	1	1	1	1	0	0	0	0	0	0	0	0

6
Etosha and the North

Etosha, the Great White Place, is regarded as one of the world's great game parks and is Namibia's prime tourist attraction. It is the home of several rare and endangered species of game, including one of the largest populations of black rhino in the world, as well as thousands of antelope. Situated a mere five hours' drive from Windhoek, the park is easily accessible from the capital and a visit can be combined with sightseeing of the numerous other tourist attractions in the area.

Long before people started roaming across the ancient landscape, dinosaurs left their footprints in the mud of what used to be an enormous lake. Evidence of these prehistoric reptiles can be seen northeast of **Omaruru**, while the fossilized remains of a prehuman hominid dating back some 13 million years were discovered in the **Otavi Mountains**. In more recent historical times the last of the Stone Age hunter–gatherers, the San, adorned the walls of the overhangs in the **Erongo Mountain** with delicate rock paintings.

The **Waterberg Plateau Park** with its sheer cliffs is a natural sanctuary to several rare and endangered species of game that can be viewed on a hiking trail or by joining a tour on an open safari vehicle. Other well-known attractions of this region include the **Hoba Meteorite** near **Grootfontein** and **Lake Otjikoto**, an enormous sinkhole near Tsumeb.

The area north of Etosha, formerly known as **Owambo**, has much potential as a tourist destination, but the creation of facilities is likely to take some time.

CLIMATE

The **dry winter** months are the best time to visit the region. Early mornings and evenings are cool, with minimum temperatures of below 5°C (41°F) being recorded at Grootfontein, but daytime temperatures are moderate. Stifling **summer** temperatures of over 30°C (86°F) are common, and **humidity** is often high. Most of the region's **rainfall**, which ranges from 350mm (14in) to 570mm (22in), is recorded between December and April. Heavy showers are accompanied by **thunderstorms**, usually in the mid-afternoon.

Opposite: *A magnificent elephant at Etosha.*

THE HERERO OF OMARURU

The history of Omaruru is
closely linked to that of the
Herero nation, and the town is
the seat of the western Herero
who settled here in the 1830s
under their Chief Zeraua. A
colourful **procession** is held
through the streets of the town
in October each year when
members of the Zeraua chief-
dom, also known as the
'White Flag' Herero, pay
tribute to their leaders. The
Franke Tower and the adjacent battlefield are a reminder
of the Uprising of 1904, which
spread to Omaruru on 17
January 1904 when the
Herero besieged the town. The
siege was relieved 20 days
later by Captain Victor Franke
after a fierce eight-hour battle.
The stone tower was erected
in 1908 to commemorate the
relief of Omaruru.

Visitors can collect a key for
the tower from the nearby
Staebe Hotel in Ian Scheepers
Street.

THE ERONGOS

The Erongo Mountain, a roughly circular massif, dominates the flat plains west of Omaruru and gives the
Erongo region its name. The mountain is an eroded
relic of a volcano that was active 140 million years ago.

The most notable rock painting here is the **'White
Elephant'** frieze in **Phillipp's Cave** on the southern edge
of the mountain, situated on the farm **Ameib**, 30km
(19 miles) from Usakos and 240km (150 miles) from
Windhoek. It is a 45-minute walk each way to view the
painting, but the scenery makes the ramble worthwhile.
Fascinating rock formations such as the **Elephant Head**
and the **Bull's Party** are also an attraction here. Ameib
is open to visitors from sunrise to sunset; an entrance
fee is charged. The guest farm also offers a variety of
accommodation, from camp sites to en-suite rooms.

Omaruru is a pleasant country town built on the
banks of the river of that name that developed around
the Rhenish mission established here in 1868. Reminders

of its early history include the **Rhenish Mission House** in Wilhelm Zeraua Street, built in 1871, which serves as a museum, and the nearby **Rhenish Mission Church**, completed in 1872. Displays in the museum include photographs of the early missionaries, old furniture and farming implements. Opening times are 08:00 to 13:00 and 14:15 to 17:00, Mondays to Fridays; collect the key from the municipal offices in Wilhelm Zeraua Street.

From Kalkfeld, 68km (42 miles) north of Omaruru, it is a 32km (20-mile) detour to the **Dinosaur Tracks**, a national monument, on the farm **Otjihaenamaperero**. An entrance fee is charged to visit the site, sunrise to sunset daily. From the parking area it is about a 10-minute walk to the sloping rock slab where the footprints of a three-toed dinosaur were deeply imbedded into the sandstone Etjo formation some 150 to 185 million years ago. Camp sites and picnic places for day visitors are available.

One of Namibia's oldest and best-known game lodges, **Mount Etjo Safari Lodge**, is situated about 34km (21 miles) east of Kalkfeld. It is named after the Etjo Mountain, a flat-topped massif, capped by sandstone of the Etjo Formation, which has resisted erosion. Accommodation is provided in luxury en suite rooms and there is an inviting swimming pool with a pool bar. Dinner is served in a *boma*. Activities include early-morning and late-afternoon game drives and guided walks. The numerous animals roaming the nature reserve include both white and black rhino, elephant and a variety of antelope. Of special interest are the lion feeds that can be viewed from the safety and comfort of a hide every evening.

Okonjima, 72km (45 miles) southwest of Otjiwarongo, is home to the AfriCat Foundation, a non-profit organization committed to the conservation of Namibia's large carnivores. Guests can visit the Foundation's cheetah pro-

Below: *The historic Franke Tower at Omaruru, an attractively embowered centre of a cattle and dairy farming region, was built in 1908 and declared a national monument in 1963. In front of the tower stands the cannon used during the battle to relieve the siege of Omaruru.*

ject, join the Cheetah Tracking trail, view leopard from the safety of a hide, or set off on guided or self-guided trails. Over 200 bird species have been recorded. Main Camp offers en-suite rooms, while accommodation at a luxury bush camp is in African-style chalets.

Above: *The pleasant pool area at the Waterberg Plateau's rest camp.*
Opposite: *The mining town of Tsumeb.*

WATERBERG TRAILS

Guided wilderness trails are conducted from a base camp in the 18,000ha (44,480 acres) wilderness area on the plateau on the second, third and fourth weekend of each month, from April through to November. Groups of six to eight people are led by an armed ranger. Trailists must bring their own food, but all other equipment is provided.

From April to November groups of 3–10 can undertake a four-day **self-guided hiking trail** covering 42km (26 miles). Trailists must be self-sufficient in all respects and, since tone can encounter potentially dangerous animals such as rhino and buffalo, hikers must be alert, fit and able to take evasive action fast.

THE WATERBERG PLATEAU PARK

Rising approximately 200m (656ft) above the surrounding plains, the Waterberg Plateau with its impressive steep-sided cliffs is also en route to Etosha. The plateau was declared a game park in 1972, and is a sanctuary to an interesting variety of game, including black and white rhino, buffalo, roan and sable antelope, as well as more common species such as giraffe, kudu, red hartebeest and eland.

Although visitors are not allowed to explore the plateau in their own vehicles, guided **game-viewing tours** are conducted every morning and afternoon. A guided **wilderness trail** and self-guided **hiking trail** are also offered, and short walks have been laid out in the rest camp, one of which leads to the top of the plateau.

The cliffs of the Waterberg are the habitat of Namibia's only breeding population of Cape vultures. Sadly, their numbers have decreased from about 500 birds in the late 1950s to a mere eight.

Amenities at the pleasant Bernabé de la Bat rest camp, which was built to blend in with the surroundings, include the historic *Rasthaus* restaurant, a shop, a filling station and a swimming pool.

Further along the B1 to Etosha is the first town north of Okahandja, **Otjiwarongo**. Of interest here is the **crocodile ranch**, started in 1985. Crocodiles are bred for their skins, which are exported to Europe where they are much in demand for the manufacture of high-quality shoes and handbags. Visitors are shown around the ranch, which is open Mondays to Fridays 09:00 to 16:00 and Saturdays, Sundays and public holidays 11:00 to 14:00.

From Otjiwarongo, the B1 leads to Otavi, Tsumeb, Namutoni in Etosha and Oshakati; the C38 gives visitors access to Damaraland and Okaukuejo in Etosha, via Outjo. On the former route a signpost about 28km (17 miles) west of Grootfontein shows the way to the **Hoba Meteorite**. The well-known attraction is about 24km (15 miles) further on along a gravel-surface road.

Grootfontein with its tree-lined streets is one of the largest towns in the north of the country and an important farming centre. Its Afrikaans name means 'large fountain' and refers to the strong springs in Tree Park. The **museum** in the historic fort off Eriksson Street has a collection of photographs depicting the history of the area, a fine collection of rocks and gems, and a display on wagon and cart manufacturing. It is open on weekdays from 09:00 to 13:00 and 14:00 to 17:00. Weekend viewing is by arrangement.

Known as 'The Gateway to Etosha', **Tsumeb** was established in 1905 by the Otavi Minen und Eisenbahn Gesellschaft (OMEG) and most of the places of interest in Tsumeb reflect the town's close links with the development of the mining industry. Buildings from this era include the **Second Director's House** in Hospital Street, the nearby **Omeg Minenbüro**, dating back to 1907, and **St Barbara's Catholic Church** in Main Road, which was built in 1913 and named after the Patron Saint of Miners.

Until its closure in late

HOBA METEORITE

With an estimated weight of 60 tonnes, the Hoba meteorite is the largest in the world. It measures 2.95m (9.7ft) by 2.84m (9.3ft) across, and its thickness varies between 122cm (48in) and 75cm (29.5in). It consists of 82.4% iron, 16.4% nickel and 0.76% cobalt, and traces of carbon, sulphur, chromium, copper and other elements. The age of the meteorite has been estimated at between 410 and 190 million years, but indications are that it fell to the earth less than 80,000 years ago.

Above: *The mysterious Lake Otjikoto, near Etosha, is actually a large sinkhole. The waters are home to the unique Otjikoto tilapia.*

RICHES FROM THE EARTH

The Tsumeb ore body was formed 600 million years ago when a bewildering variety of minerals were injected into an underground cavity. Forty of the 213 minerals contained in the ore body were found only at Tsumeb. The mine was renowned for its magnificent specimens of secondary copper minerals such as azurite and dioptase, and spectacular crystals of mimetite and wulfenite. Some fine specimens of minerals from the mine are displayed in the **Tsumeb Museum** in Main Street, but unfortunately the most comprehensive collection is in the Smithsonian Institute Museum of Natural History in Washington.

1997, the Tsumeb Mine was a major producer of copper and lead, while silver, cadmium, zinc and arsenic trioxide were produced as by-products. The smelter produces blister copper and refined lead from other mines.

The **Tsumeb Museum** in Main Street is housed in the old German school and exhibits minerals from the Tsumeb Mine. There is an excellent collection of armaments abandoned by the German forces in Lake Otjikoto in 1915 – some of the items on display are several beautifully restored cannons, ammunition carriers and machine guns. Opening times for the museum are 09:00 to 12:00 and 15:00 to 18:00 on weekdays, and 15:00 to 18:00 on Saturdays.

About 24km (15 miles) from Tsumeb is another well-known tourist attraction, **Lake Otjikoto**. The lake is a sinkhole formed by underground water that dissolved the dolomite rock to form a huge cavern, the roof of which subsequently collapsed.

The endangered *Otjikoto tilapia* is found here and in only one other place, the nearby Lake Guinas. This species reaches a length of up to 14cm (5.5 in) and varies in colour from dark greenish-black to a combination of white, black, yellow and blue.

In 1915 the retreating German forces dumped their armaments in the lake rather than let them fall in the hands of the advancing South African forces. Several of the armaments have been recovered and are on display in the Khorab Room at the Tsumeb Museum.

Another sunken lake, **Guinas**, is situated southwest of Otjikoto, but since it is a 50km (31 miles) return trip from the main road, it is usually bypassed. Visitors with time on hand will find the detour rewarding as Guinas is not only deeper than Otjikoto but it is also far more scenic.

ETOSHA NATIONAL PARK

Centred on the vast Etosha Pan with its shimmering mirages, the renowned Etosha National Park is one of the world's greatest conservation areas. It is a sanctuary to large herds of animals typical of the African plains, and entices tourists hoping to spot four of the 'big five' – lion, elephant, leopard and rhino. After the summer rains thousands of waterbirds are attracted to the seasonally inundated pans and vleis.

Covering 22,270km² (8,598 sq miles), Etosha stretches for about 300km (186 miles) from west to east and 110km (68 miles) from north to south at its widest point.

The western part of the park has not been developed for tourism and as the animals are not used to vehicles, species such as lions and elephants tend to be aggressive. Tourists cannot visit this section of the park individually, only with a tour operator registered by the Ministry of Environment and Tourism.

Entry permits are necessary. There are three entrance gates to the park: Von Lindequist near Namutoni, Andersson near Okaukuejo, and Nehale lya Mpingana on the northern boundary near Andoni Waterhole.

Warning: Only leave your vehicle in designated places, and keep a respectful distance from elephants, especially lone bulls and cows with calves. Never feed wild animals and do not sleep in the open in rest camps.

ETOSHA PAN

The white clay pan covers about 5000 km² (1930.5 sq miles), or nearly 25% of the park's surface. It is often dry for decades, but the flood waters of the Ekuma and Oshigambo rivers in the north and the Owambo River in the east occasionally inundate the pan, creating a vast, shallow inland lake. Although the salinity of the water is twice as high as that of sea water, the shallow water creates ideal conditions for the growth of blue-green algae, which provides a feeding ground for up to a million flamingoes in years with good rains. The pan is classified as a saline desert and, with the exception of a hardy, salt-loving grass, it supports hardly any other vegetation when it is dry.

Left: *An elephant visits guests at Etosha's Okaukuejo. The camp boasts a viewing platform and a floodlit water hole.*

Below: *The historic fort at the Namutoni rest camp.*

Accommodation

The eastern section of the park is traversed by a network of more than 700km (435 miles) of tourist roads, and accommodation is provided in three rest camps, Okaukuejo in the west, Halali in the centre and Namutoni in the east. The accommodation ranges from thatched bungalows to rooms in the historic Fort Namutoni and camp sites. Amenities at each camp include a restaurant serving breakfast, lunch and dinner, a shop that stocks groceries, curios and liquor, a filling station and a swimming pool.

Each of the three rest camps has a distinctive atmosphere. **Okaukuejo**, 18km (11 miles) from the Andersson Gate in the south, was originally used as a Police post and is the oldest rest camp in the park. A characteristic feature of the camp is the limestone water tower, which affords stunning views of the surrounding plains. An attraction at Okaukuejo is the floodlit water hole just outside the perimeter of the camp.

Halali rest camp, midway between Okaukuejo and Namutoni, is surrounded by dense mopane woodlands near Tsumasa Hill, a small dolomite outcrop. A short walk has been laid out against the hill and the view from the top is especially beautiful at sunset. The lower slopes of the hill overlook a floodlit water hole.

The central feature of **Namutoni**, just 12km (7.5 miles) from the Von Lindequist Gate in the east, is the picturesque old fort with its whitewashed walls. Here too visitors can watch the animals drinking at a water hole just outside the camp's perimeter. Of Etosha's three rest camps, the camp site at Namutoni is undoubtedly the most pleasant.

Wildlife ★★★

Although the park is the habitat of about 114 mammal species, the average visitor is unlikely to see more than 20 species. The attraction of Etosha is not its diversity of species or large numbers of game, but the relative ease with which a variety of game can be seen, especially during the dry winter months. During the rainy season, however, the animals disperse widely throughout the park until the diminishing field water forces them to concentrate in the vicinity of the water holes.

Etosha's **lion** population has decreased from over 500 in 1981 to an estimated 190–265, but these magnificent animals are still often seen near water holes, especially during the dry winter months. **Cheetah** and **leopard** are less frequently spotted.

Elephants are commonly sighted, but their numbers fluctuate considerably as many migrate out of the park during the wet season.

Giraffe are plentiful throughout the park, while the smaller **black-backed jackal** and **ground squirrel** are also likely to be seen. **Spotted hyena** and **warthog** are two other mammals to look out for.

Etosha has the largest population of the southwestern subspecies of the black rhino in the world, totalling over

Above: *Etosha has a large resident population of lion, Africa's largest predator.*

LIONS ON THE PILL

During the early 1980s it became apparent that Etosha's exploding lion population (numbering about 500) would have to be controlled. As an alternative to culling, a unique population control experiment was conducted by implanting a slow-releasing hormonal capsule into the neck muscles of 10 lionesses. No differences were observed between the behaviour of treated and untreated lionesses, but while the implants were in place, none of the 10 treated lionesses fell pregnant. When the contraceptives were removed, they became pregnant within 36 days.

800 animals. They are often seen at the floodlit water hole at Okaukuejo, as well as in the Halali area. **White rhino** were reintroduced into the park in 1995 after they became locally extinct nearly a century earlier.

Springbok are the most numerous **antelope** and during summer and early autumn they congregrate in herds of several hundred on the open plains, while several thousand gemsbok and Burchell's zebra also roam the plains. Other antelope include eland, red hartebeest and kudu, as well as steenbok and common duiker.

Although fencing the park has created a sanctuary for the animals, migratory species such as the **blue wildebeest** have been affected adversely. During the late 1950s Etosha's blue wildebeest population numbered over 25,000, but as a result of the disruption of their migration route, anthrax and competition with other plains animals, their numbers declined to fewer than 2200 in the early 1980s. Numbers now range between 3400 and 5900.

The diversity of habitats attracts a wide variety of **birds** and to date about 392 species have been recorded. After the summer rains have set in, a number of migrants from the northern hemisphere join the resident species. Fischer's Pan near Namutoni attracts a large variety of waterbirds and in years of exceptionally good rainfall Etosha Pan attracts up to a million flamingoes. Species likely to be of interest to birders include the bare-cheeked babbler, often seen at Halali, and the black-faced babbler, recorded in the woodlands of eastern Etosha. The crowned crane may be sighted on the Andoni Plains, north of Namutoni, after summer rains, where bird-watchers should also keep an eye out for blue crane and clapper lark.

Left: *Giraffe, kneeling awkwardly to drink, are most vulnerable to predators when at a water hole. They usually take their fill one at a time while the others keep watch.*
Opposite: *An Etosha gemsbok slakes its thirst. Both sexes of this hardy antelope have rapier-like horns which, seen in profile, may have given rise to the legend of the unicorn. The animals have been known to kill attacking lions by impaling them.*

Vegetation

The **vegetation** of Etosha is dominated by mopane savanna and woodlands, while the edge of the pan is fringed by dwarf shrub savannas, except in the west where it is bordered by grassland which attracts thousands of antelope after the summer rains. Sandwiched between the dwarf shrub savannas and the mopane savanna and woodlands to the south of the pan is a narrow strip of grassland which is utilized as a winter grazing area. Several other vegetation types can also be distinguished – a few kilometres south of Namutoni the vegetation is dominated by tall, dense tamboti and purple-pod terminalia woodlands, while the vegetation of the northeastern corner of the park consists of a mixed tree and shrub savanna.

PRIVATE GAME RESERVES

In recent years a number of luxury game lodges have been opened close to the park's two entrance gates. **Onguma Game Reserve** adjoining Fischer's Pan on the eastern boundary has a diversity of game and offers a variety of accomodation.

  Mokuti Lodge, near the eastern entrance gate to the park, is rated as one of Namibia's top hotels. Mokuti means 'in the bush' in the Owambo language, and,

MORINGA TREE

The hardy moringa tree, known also as the phantom tree, usually grows on rocky slopes. **Tsumasa Hill** in Halali rest camp is a typical habitat of the moringa, and here visitors can closely inspect the tree. However, at the **Moringa Forest**, west of Okaukuejo, several hundred of these trees grow on the open plains. The moringa usually has a straight, upright trunk, but those growing at the Moringa Forest are grotesquely shaped with gnarled trunks, while some have several trunks – hence this is often called the Haunted Forest or the Ghost Forest. The weird shapes of the trees have been attributed to browsing by giraffe and elephant.

Above: *Game-viewing from an open vehicle.*
Opposite: *A cuca shop in northern Namibia.*

WATER HOLES OF ETOSHA

In addition to constructed drinking places (water holes), there are three types of natural springs that provide water for the wildlife in the park. Along the edge of the pan there are several **contact springs** which are created by water seeping through the calcrete and then being forced to the surface when it reaches the underlying impermeable clay. **Water-level springs** are usually associated with limestone and are found in places where the water table is higher than the ground level. In some areas (usually on top of limestone outcrops), water is forced upwards under pressure to form **artesian springs**.

---

appropriately, the rustic, thatched bungalows blend in well with the vegetation.

Accommodation ranges from single to family and luxury units with en suite facilities, and all units are air conditioned. Guests can view game, including giraffe, kudu and gemsbok, on foot by following self-guided walking routes, while a variety of reptiles can be seen in the **Ontouka Reptile Park**. Situated close to the lodge complex, it is open daily from sunrise to sunset. The lodge also has a swimming pool.

Also located near the eastern gate is **Etosha Aoba Lodge**, built amidst the 7000ha (17,300-acre) **Fischer's Pan Private Game Reserve** bordering on the Etosha National Park in the west. The reserve is home to a rich diversity of game, with antelope such as blue wildebeest, kudu and springbok, as well as giraffe, leopard and hyena. Visitors are accommodated in ten thatched cottages (with en-suite facilities) shaded by tamboti trees.

Situated quite close to the southern entrance to the park is the luxurious **Ongava Lodge**, built on a dolomite outcrop. A central feature of the lodge is the enormous thatched dining area overlooking the surrounding savannas and a small water hole that attracts game during the dry season. Accommodation is provided in the 10 thatched bungalows, each with en suite facilities and air conditioning. Each unit has its own balcony overlooking the reserve, and the lodge has a swimming pool. Guests can also opt to stay in a luxury tented camp in the wilderness camp.

Activities offered include game drives to Etosha, as well as guided walks and night drives in the 35,000ha (86,500 acres) Ongava Game Reserve.

The North

North of Etosha the landscape is dominated by an exceptionally flat plain that is covered by a network of shallow watercourses, known as *oshanas*, in the central area. Formerly known as Owambo, the area has been divided into four regions: **Omusati** in the west, the central **Oshana** region, **Ohangwena** and **Oshikoto**.

With a total population of about 650,000 people, northern Namibia is the most densely populated area in the country. About three-quarters of the people live in the rural areas where they practise crop production and livestock farming. The most important crops cultivated are millet, locally known as *mahangu*, sorghum and beans, while cattle farming is another important agricultural activity. Owambo women are skilled at basketry, and baskets, pottery and handmade musical instruments can be bought from roadside stalls in the region.

Oshakati, **Ongwediva** and **Ondangwa**, the only major towns north of Etosha, are unlike any other settlements in Namibia. They are a hive of activity with people thronging around the open-air stalls along the main roads and taxis careering along the roads at breakneck speed. Stray cattle, donkeys and goats pose a threat to motorists, so be alert, even in the towns.

Attractions include the historic Finnish mission complex at **Olukonda**, 13km south of Ondangwa. It comprises the historic mission house, the mission church dating back to 1889, the Nakambale Museum and a traditional Ndonga homestead. The accommodation ranges from a missionary cottage to camp sites and traditional huts. The gigantic **Ombalantu baobab tree** at Outapi (the are also camp sites available) and the royal homestead at Tsandi are also worth a visit.

Cuca Shops

A familiar feature of the north are the thousands of informal trading stores, known as *cuca* shops. The name was originally adopted by shops on the Angolan border that sold Angolan beer of that name, but is now used throughout the north. The square, tin-roofed buildings are usually painted in bright colours and are given way-out names like, 'Jamaica Inn' or 'Love Station'. Basic commodities and liquor are sold, and they close when the last customers leave.

Etosha and the North at a Glance

April to **September** is most popular – cooler temperatures are pleasant for game-viewing and hiking. Dry winter months of **May** to **September** are best for game-viewing in Etosha as animals congregate around water holes. **Summer** is best for bird-watching as numerous migrant species visit the pans after summer rains.

Air Namibia, tel: (061) 2996444, fax: 2996168, has regular **scheduled flights** to Ondangwa.
There are **landing strips** at all three rest camps in Etosha, at Mount Etjo Safari Lodge and at Ongava Lodge.
For **air charter** contact (Windhoek) Comav, tel: (061) 227512, fax: 245612; Desert Air, tel: (061) 228101, fax: 248316; Westair, tel: (061) 221091, fax: 232778.
All major towns in the region are connected to Windhoek by a **tarred road**. Intercape Mainliner, tel: (061) 227847, has a **coach** to Victoria Falls via Otavi and Grootfontein on Mondays and Fridays.

The region is served by an excellent **road network** and all tourist attractions are accessible by car (except some parts of the north).
Gravel-surface roads usually in good condition.
Car hire from Avis at Tsumeb,

Jordan Street, tel: (067) 220520, fax: 220821; Mokuti Lodge (by prior arrangement), tel: (067) 220520, fax: 220821; Imperial, 1551 Omeg Allee, Tsumeb, tel: (067) 220728, fax: 220916. Further north, cars and **four-wheel-drive** vehicles can be hired from Santorini Car Hire in Oshakati, tel: (065) 220506. TransNamib offers three **passenger train** services a week between Windhoek/ Walvis Bay, Otjiwarongo and Tsumeb, tel: (061) 2982032.

Kalkfeld
Mount Etjo Safari Lodge, near Kalkfeld: excellent accommodation and service, guided walks, game-viewing drives and viewing of nightly lion feeds; accommodation in en suite rooms, and the lodge has a swimming pool with a pool bar, tel: (067) 290174, fax: 290172.

Omaruru
Ameib Ranch, foot of Erongo Mountain: offers accommodation in a farmhouse and camp sites; attractions include rock paintings in Phillip's Cave and interesting rock formations, tel: (064) 530803.
Ekapo Game Lodge, near Omaruru: offers accommodation in bungalows, game-viewing drives and walking trails, tel: (064) 570551, fax: 570553.
Erongo Wilderness Lodge,

10km (6 miles) west of Omaruru in Erongo Mountains: luxury tents under thatch raised on platforms, nature walks and drives, rock paintings and good birding, tel: (064) 570537, fax: 570536.

Ondangwa
Cresta Lodge Pandu Ondangwa, near centre of business district: three-star hotel, air-conditioned rooms with en-suite facilities, restaurant, bar and swimming pool, tel: (065) 241900, fax: 241919.

Oshakati
Santorini Inn: has en suite rooms, a restaurant, bar and swimming pool, tel: (065) 220457.
Oshakati Country Lodge: luxury en suite double rooms, restaurant, bar and swimming pool, tel: (061) 374750.

Otjiwarongo
Okonjima Guest Lodge, 70km (44 miles) from Otjiwarongo: offers en suite accommodation in double rooms, good food served in a dining area under thatch and a relaxed atmosphere; activities offered include guided walks, cheetah and leopard feeds, bird-watching and viewing of nocturnal animals, tel: (067) 304563.

Outjo
Ongava Lodge, near southern entrance to Etosha: has thatched chalets with en suite facilities, a large thatched

Etosha and the North at a Glance

lounge/dining room and swimming pool, and a luxury tented camp; activities include day or night game-viewing drives in open safari vehicles and guided walks, tel: (061) 274500.
Etosha Gateway Lodge, near southern entrance to Etosha: provides reasonably priced, a restaurant and a swimming pool, tel: (067) 333440.

Tsumeb
Mokuti Lodge, near eastern boundary of Etosha: en suite accommodation, restaurant, swimming pool with a pool bar, tel and fax: (067) 229084.
Etosha Aoba Lodge, near the eastern boundary of Etosha: thatched chalets, guided nature drives and walks, tel: (067) 229106, fax: 229107.

Tariffs at all **lodges** and **guest farms** are inclusive of three meals a day. The **Onduli Dining Room** at Mokuti Lodge offers excellent buffet meals with a variety of game dishes.
Etosha National Park offers buffet meals in the restaurants in the three rest camps.
The **Bäckerei & Café Jakob**, Okavango Street, Grootfontein has the best German confectionery in the north of the country and a tea or lunch stop is highly recommended.
In the north, **Cresta Lodge** in Ondangwa has a restaurant, and **Santorini Inn** and the **Oshakati Country Lodge** in Oshakati both have restaurants.

Tours of Etosha National Park: Early-morning and late-afternoon game-viewing drives from Mokuti Lodge to the Etosha National Park. Etosha Fly-In Safaris, based at Tsumeb, also offers a fully inclusive fly-in service to Etosha National Park, tel: (067) 220574, fax: 220832.
Waterberg Plateau Park: guided game-viewing tours in open four-wheel-drive vehicles are conducted twice a day; in addition, guided three-day wilderness trails are conducted weekly between April and November.
Tours of Etosha, with additional scheduled stops at Lake Otjikoto and Tsumeb, are offered by Sense of Africa, tel: (061) 275300. The Namib Travel Shop, tel: (061) 274500, offers **fly-in safaris to Etosha**. If you are intending to go off and explore off-the-beaten-track destinations in the north of the country, it is advisable to purchase **topographical maps** of the area from the Surveyor General, on the corner of Robert Mugabe Avenue and Dr AB May Street, Windhoek; the **Automobile Association**

(AA), situated on the corner of Independence Avenue and Fidel Castro Street, Windhoek, tel: (061) 224201, provides travel information for members.

A wide variety of books showcasing the Etosha area is available at the three rest camps in the park. Here is a select list:
Etosha National Park by David Rogers; useful compact guide in full colour.
Sasol Birds of Southern Africa by Ian Sinclair; comprehensive, full-colour guide.
Field Guide to the Mammals of Southern Africa by Chris and Tilde Stuart; informative, with colour photographs.

Grootfontein Museum, tel: (067) 242456.
Namibia Wildlife Resorts, Windhoek, tel: (061) 236975.
Museum at Omaruru, contact the municipality, tel: (064) 570028.
Namibia Tourism, Windhoek, tel: (061) 2906000, fax: 254848.
Tsumeb Tourism Centre, tel: (067) 220728.

ETOSHA PAN	J	F	M	A	M	J	J	A	S	O	N	D
AVERAGE TEMP. °F	79	77	75	73	66	61	61	66	73	79	79	79
AVERAGE TEMP. °C	26	25	24	23	19	16	16	19	23	26	26	26
HOURS OF SUN DAILY	8	7	8	9	10	10	10	10	9	9	9	10
RAINFALL in	3	4	3	1	1	0	0	0	0	0	1	2.5
RAINFALL mm	75	109	75	26	18	1	0	0	2	7	31	68
DAYS OF RAINFALL	15	13	11	6	1	0	0	0	1	5	9	13

7
Kavango and Caprivi

Northeastern Namibia, with its woodlands, rivers and swamps, is unlike any other part of the country, and is usually a complete surprise to the first-time visitor.

Nyae Nyae, previously eastern Bushmanland, is home to the Ju!Wasi San (Bushmen) who have lived here for thousands of years. Do not expect to see the Bushman portrayed in coffee-table books, though; the Ju!Wasi are a people in transition, determined to control their future.

To the north lie the **Kavango** and the **Khaudum Game Park**, sanctuary to the rare roan antelope, the endangered wild dog and several other species of game. The rest camp at **Popa Falls** and the nearby **Mahango Game Park** are two other well-known attractions in this area.

Namibia's easternmost region, the **Caprivi**, is largely unexplored by tourists. One of the area's attractions is its prolific bird life, and nearly 70% of Namibia's bird species, many of which do not occur elsewhere, have been recorded here. Another drawcard is the rivers that can be explored by boat, and tiger fishing is popular too. **Katima Mulilo**, the main settlement, is the gateway to Victoria Falls in Zimbabwe and Chobe National Park in Botswana.

The parks and communal conservancies in the Caprivi offer visitors an opportunity to experience the wilderness atmosphere of northeastern Namibia and facilities range from very basic camp sites to community-run facilities. The camp sites are unfenced and visitors should be aware at all times of the potential danger posed by wild animals.

Northeastern Namibia is a **malaria** endemic area, and the waterways are infested with **bilharzia** (*see* page 126).

DON'T MISS

★★★ Popa Falls: a 1km (0.6 miles) wide series of rapids in unsurpassed surroundings.
★★ Mahango Game Park: prolific bird life and antelope species rarely seen elsewhere in Namibia.
★★ Mudumu National Park: delightful scenery and game.
★★ Mamili National Park: magnificent scenery and aquatic and semi-aquatic animals in the Linyanti Swamps.

Opposite: *Lianshulu Lodge guests study wildlife from a raft on the Kwando River in East Caprivi.*

BUSHMANLAND

This region is a 1,800,000ha (4,447,893 acres) wilderness of woodlands, large baobab trees, seasonally inundated pans and open plains. Tsumkwe, administrative centre of the area, is the only large settlement; here visitors can purchase basic necessities, but no petrol is available.

The western two-thirds of the area is largely uninhabited, except for settlements at former South African Defence Force bases where !Kung San refugees from southern Angola were resettled in 1978.

Nyae Nyae (formerly known as Eastern Bushmanland) is the last stronghold of the **Ju!Wasi** who, just three decades ago, were the last of the independent hunter-gatherers in southern Africa. As a result of influences their traditional way of life collapsed permanently in the early 1970s. Today their total population in the Nyae Nyae area consists of about 3000 people living in 32 communities, and they are adapting to a new way of life.

Proclaimed in 1998 as the first communal conservancy in Namibia, the Nyae Nyae Conservancy covers some 900,000ha (2,223,900 acres) of tree savanna, woodlands and pans situated to the south and east of Tsumkwe. Enormous baobabs are a conspicuous feature of the Nyae Nyae area. Near the settlement of

TIPS FOR CAMPING IN BUSHMANLAND

• Be courteous and show respect for the Ju!Wasi culture.
• Keep to the tracks; off-road driving damages plants that the Ju!Wasi gather.
• Camping is only allowed in designated areas.
• Do not litter.
• Ensure that fires are completely burnt out.
• Ask permission to take photos of people.

Djökhoe the **Holboom** (Hollow Tree) with its hollow trunk and several other enormous baobabs growing amidst the woodlands are notable.

Game is not as abundant as in Khaudum, but during the dry season you could spot elephant, giraffe, roan antelope, warthog and wild dog, or even lion, leopard and hyena. Between December and May the seasonally inundated pans can cover up to a fifth of Nyae Nyae, attracting thousands of waterbirds. Camping is only allowed at designated camp sites. These include **Djökhoe**, lying to the southeast of Tsumkwe, and Makuri, which is located close to Makuri Pan, offering good birding opportunities of especially waterfowl when the pan holds water.

Except for the major gravel-surface road that leads eastwards from the B8 to Tsumkwe and the Botswana border and a few proclaimed roads in western Bushmanland, most of the roads are mere tracks. The area is accessible only by four-wheel-drive vehicle, and some tracks are impassable during the rainy season.

Below: *A Bushman of the Nyae Nyae area near Tsumkwe. Namibia's 34,000 San people, or Bushmen, wandering hunter–gatherers by tradition, are much more sedentary than their forbears.*

The turn-off to another well-known baobab, the **Dorslandboom** (Thirstland Trek Tree), is reached about 37km (23 miles) northeast of Tsumkwe on the track to Khaudum. The Thirstland Trekkers camped here in 1892 during their epic journey from the Transvaal to Angola.

KAVANGO

This region takes its name from the Kavango River, which forms Namibia's border with Angola for about 400km (248.5 miles). The river is the lifeblood of the region and nearly 75% of the people live alongside or close to it.

Khaudum Game Park

North of Bushmanland is the **Khaudum Game Park**, a 384,000ha

(948,884 acres) sanctuary for a variety of animals, including elephant, roan, lion and the wild dog.

There are two rest camps; Sikeretti in the south and Khaudum in the north, but only camping has been allowed since late 2005 as the wood and thatch huts were in need of renovations. No reservations are required and fees must be paid on arrival. Enquire from Namibia Wildlife Resorts about the reopening of the rest camps.

Although the park has a well-developed network of tracks, the sandy terrain can only be negotiated by a four-wheel-drive vehicle. Because of the remoteness of the area, it is essential to travel in a party of at least two vehicles and to carry sufficient emergency supplies.

Rundu

Situated on the southern bank of the Kavango River, **Rundu** is the administrative centre of the Kavango region. There is little of interest to the tourist here, but the **Mbanguru Woodcarvers' Co-operative** is worth a stop on your way through the town. The Kavango people are skilled woodcarvers and items on sale range from animal carvings to wooden spoons, jewellery chests and dining-room tables and chairs. Teak is mainly used, and faces are a popular motif.

From Rundu the B2 heads in an easterly direction,

RARE ANTELOPE

Northeastern Namibia is the habitat of several semi-aquatic antelope species not found elsewhere in the country's conservation areas. **Waterbuck** can usually be seen on the floodplains and grassy areas along the rivers, while the **red lechwe** is attracted to the floodplains and shallow water. The **sitatunga** is another semi-aquatic species, but since it favours papyrus swamps it is seen only infrequently. The very rare **puku**, a species that favours dry, grassy flood-plains, used to occur in the Mamili National Park, but has become locally extinct.

Right: *Exploring the Kavango by river-boat.*

passing through dense woodlands dominated by teak trees, and reaches Divundu after about 200km (124 miles). This entire stretch is tarred.

Popa Falls ★★★

The rest camp at **Popa Falls**, a short distance beyond Divundu along the gravel-surface road to Botswana, is a welcome refuge on a hot day. The rustic, thatched bungalows are shaded by tall trees and the sound of the continuous gushing of the nearby cascades provides a background for the melodious calls of a rich variety of birds. There is also a grass camp site with a field kitchen and ablution facilities. As there is no restaurant, visitors must be self-sufficient. Contact Namibia Wildlife Resorts for reservations and information.

The 'falls' consists of a network of rushing channels, water courses and small islands that form a spectacular 1km (0.6 miles) wide series of rapids where the Kavango River breaks through a quartzite barrier. However, only a small section of this spectacle can be seen from the southern bank of the river. The **Popa Falls** is best viewed between July and October when the level of the river is low.

Visitors should not swim in the river because of the very real danger presented by crocodiles and hippos, and as some parts of the river are bilharzia-infested.

Mahango Game Reserve ★★

The relatively small 25,000ha (61,775 acres) **Mahango Game Reserve,** comprising woodlands, floodplains and grassy, seasonally inundated river courses, lies at the upper end of the Panhandle of the renowned Okavango Delta in Botswana. Although there is no accommodation in the park, the Popa Falls rest camp and several other establishments are conveniently close by. The park is open throughout the year between sunrise and sunset, and entry permits can be obtained at the gate.

There are two **circular drives** that give visitors the opportunity to explore the area. The route winding alongside the Kavango River is suitable for cars and

---

BIRDS OF NORTHEASTERN NAMIBIA

Several bird species are found only in this area or have a limited distribution elsewhere in Namibia. Species likely to be of interest to birders include the slaty egret, longtoed lapwing, African skimmer and coppery-tailed coucal. Among the noteworthy species of the riverine forest are the western banded snake eagle and Hartlaub's babbler, and the copper sunbird has been recorded at Lianshulu. The greater swamp warbler is found only in the papyrus swamps, while Bradfield's hornbill and the greater blue-eared starling can be seen in the woodlands.

CLIMATE

The climate in the northeast is subtropical. From **April** to **August** it is dry and cool with occasional **frost** and minimum temperatures of below 6°C (42.8°F). From **September** to **November** it is **hot** and **dry** with an average maximum of 35°C (95°F). The **rainy season** is from early **December** to **March/April** when 500-700mm (19.5–27.5in) rain falls as violent **thunderstorms** and temperatures and **humidity** are unpleasantly high.

affords visitors good views of the grassy floodplains
where red lechwe, reedbuck and waterbuck can be
seen grazing during the early mornings. Chobe bushbuck favour the dense riverine forests, while you can
look out for the elusive sitatunga in the papyrus
swamps. A picnic site on the riverbank of the Kavango
is a good vantage point for bird-watching

Mahango is renowned for its large numbers of
elephants, and during the dry season they are often
encountered close to the river. Other animals to look out
for include tsessebe, roan antelope, sable, impala and
buffalo, while lion occasionally pass through the area.

The route south of the road heading to the Botswana
border winds across the dunes and is negotiable by four-
wheel-drive vehicle only. One of the main attractions of
this area is its prolific bird life, and to date some 440 bird
species have been recorded here. Since many of these are
migrants, summer is the most rewarding time to visit.

Visitors may walk around in the park, but bear in
mind that wild animals roam around freely, so it is not
safe to venture too far from your vehicle.

The Mahango Game Park is to be incorporated into
the proposed Bwabwata National Park.

West Caprivi

West Caprivi, a 32km (20 miles) wide ribbon of dense
woodlands, links Kavango and East Caprivi. Known in
colonial times as the Caprivi Zipfel, now often called
the Caprivi Strip, this geographical curiosity stretches
for 200km (124 miles) between the Kavango River in
the west and the Kwando in the east. In the south it is
bounded by Botswana and in the north by Angola.

Bwabwata National Park

The proposed Bwabwata National Park will involve the
merger of the Caprivi and Mahango game parks and the
incorporation of the 20,000ha (49,420-acre) Golden
Triangle at the eastern end of the Caprivi Strip. To enable
the San people living in the Caprivi Game Park to continue living in the new park, the settlements of Bagani

and Omega will be deproclaimed from the park. The new park will have core conservation areas at Mahango and Buffalo in the west and Kwando in the east, while the central area will be a multiple land-use area.

With a bird list of over 340 species in the Caprivi Game Park and a possible 70 other species, the park is rich in bird life. Among the game to be seen are elephant, hippo, buffalo, impala, roan, sable, tsessebe, reedbuck, lion, leopard and wild dog.

Access is restricted to the Kwando Triangle which has a network of tracks. There are community-run camp sites at Nambwa and Bum Hill.

Susuwe Island Lodge

Built on a small island in the Kwando River, Susuwe is the sister to Impalila Island Lodge, an upmarket establishment offering superb service. Guests stay in luxury chalets with *en suite* facilities, a wooden deck and private plunge pool. There is also a large deck where meals are served and a tree-top viewing deck built around an ancient sausage tree. Activities include early morning nature walks and boat trips on the Kwando River, as well as afternoon game drives with sundowners served in the middle of the bush. Situated in the Kwando Triangle, the lodge offers good game-viewing, especially during the dry season, and superb birding opportunities. It is aimed primarily at the fly-in market.

Below: *The enchanting malachite kingfisher, a familiar sight in the watery world of Caprivi.*

EAST CAPRIVI

Kongola is the gateway to **East Caprivi**, a water-rich region of floodplains bounded on all sides by rivers (the

BEST BUYS

• **Kavango woodcarvings** from Mbanguru Co-operative in Rundu, or along the main road south of Rundu.
• **Bushman handicrafts** from San people living in Nyae Nyae.
• **Zambian and Caprivian handicrafts** such as wood and stone carvings, baskets, printed fabric and African-style clothing from the Caprivi Art Centre.
• **Caprivian handicrafts** like baskets, wood and stone carvings, and pottery from Lizauli Traditional Village.

Below: *Local art, handicrafts and African fashions are on display at the Caprivi Art Centre.*

Kwando, Linyanti and Chobe), except for its northern boundary with Zambia. A 120km (75 miles) tarred road links Kongola and Katima Mulilo, but a four-wheel-drive vehicle is essential to visit the off-the-beaten-track attractions in the region.

Mudumu National Park ★★

The Kwando River with its tranquil lagoons, narrow slow-flowing channels and magnificent riverine forests forms the western boundary of this unspoilt conservation area and is an ideal habitat for hippo and crocodiles, as well as small numbers of red lechwe, reedbuck and the water-adapted sitatunga. The remainder of the 100,000ha (247,105 acres) **Mudumu National Park** is dominated by mopane woodlands where elephant, buffalo, impala, kudu, giraffe and Burchell's zebra, as well as the rare roan antelope and sable, roam. The park, which is accessible only by four-wheel-drive vehicle, is a bird-watcher's paradise and chances are that you could spot several species that do not occur elsewhere in Namibia. Look out for the distinctive African fish eagle,

Pel's fishing owl and the Narina trogon. Basic facilities are available at Nakatwa. Contact the Ministry of Environment and Tourism in Katima Mulilo for permits.

Lianshulu Lodge is situated on the banks of the Kwando River in the Mudumu National Park and is accessible by car. The lodge overlooks the quiet back-waters of Lianshulu Lagoon and guests are accommodated in reed-and-thatch chalets with en suite facilities. There is also a thatched dining area, as well as a swimming pool. Among the variety of activities offered are guided walks, game-viewing drives and a leisurely sunset cruise on the Kwando River. Nearby **Lianshulu Bush Lodge** imparts an atmosphere of being out in the bush.

Visitors to the park can gain an insight into local traditions by visiting the **Lizauli Traditional Village** just outside the park boundaries. The programme is aimed at uplifting the local community and enabling them to share in the benefits of tourism.

Above: *Women grinding millet at Lizauli Traditional Village.*

Mamili National Park ★★

The focal point of the **Mamili National Park**, 30km (19 miles) south of Mudumu, are the **Linyanti Swamps**. When the level of the Kwando River is high, as was the case in 1958 and 1978, the floodplain grasslands are transformed into reed-lined channels, forested islands and vast reed and papyrus swamps.

More than three-quarters of the park is inaccessible when the Kwando River spills over its banks, usually in June, inundating large areas. Once the floods have subsided, however, it is possible to reach Nkasa and Lupala islands which lie at the heart of the 32,000ha (79,075 acres) park, and during the dry season Mamili is accessible by four-wheel-drive vehicle. Note that facilities are limited

ANGLING

The rivers of northeastern Namibia are the habitat of more than 70 species of fish and offer excellent angling opportunities. The tiger fish is undoubtly one of the best sporting fish in the world and trophies of over 10kg (22lb) are possible on the Zambezi River. Although fishing is possible all year round, between August and December is generally the best time to catch tiger fish. Bream, a popular eating fish, and nembwe of up to 4kg (9lb) are also caught, while barbel of up to 20kg (44lb) can be landed.

EXCURSIONS TO ZIMBABWE AND BOTSWANA

Victoria Falls in Zimbabwe and Botswana's Chobe National Park are just 195km (121 miles) and 70km (43.7 miles) from Katima Mulilo, and easily accessible by car.

The 1.7km (1-mile) wide **Victoria Falls** is most impressive after the rainy season, towards the end of summer. Plunging an average of 92m (302ft), the cascade causes a mist spray that has resulted in the beautiful rain forest flanking the Falls. The thundering sound and the mist gave rise to the local name *Mosi-oa-Tunya*, which means 'the smoke that thunders'.

Chobe National Park in northern Botswana is renowned for the luxury Chobe Game Lodge close to Kasane and its herds of elephant. Other game includes Chobe bushbuck, sable, roan, hippo, lion, cheetah and wild dog.

to three basic camp sites, and visitors must be totally self-sufficient, which includes bringing along your own water and firewood. Contact the Ministry of Environment and Tourism in Katima Mulilo for permits, camp site reservations and information.

Game to be seen includes large herds of elephant and buffalo, lion, leopard, spotted hyena, hippo, giraffe, impala, red lechwe, reedbuck and the elusive sitatunga. With noteworthy species such as wattled crane, rosy-throated longclaw, slaty egret, Meves' starling and greater swamp warbler, the park also offers outstanding birding.

Katima Mulilo

The administrative centre of the Caprivi region, **Katima Mulilo**, lies on the banks of the mighty Zambezi River, which forms the boundary with Zambia. The wide, slow-flowing river, fringed by tall trees, is inhabited by animals such as hippos and crocodiles, and keen birders will be quite delighted with the variety of species that can be ticked off your birding list on a short walk along the Zambezi.

The **open-air market**, where dried fish, live chickens and printed cloth are just a few of the wares traded, is worth visiting, even if only to experience the hive of activity. Souvenir-hunters should also visit the **Caprivi Art Centre** where a selection of wood and soapstone carvings, baskets and ethnic clothing featuring colourful African prints can be purchased.

Katima, is a convenient base from which to explore the waterways and game parks of East Caprivi, while the Chobe National Park in Botswana and Zimbabwe's Victoria Falls are just a few hours' drive away.

The **Zambezi Lodge**, on the outskirts of the town along the banks of the Zambezi River, is known for its floating bar from where superb views can be enjoyed as you sip a sundowner. The riverine trees are rewarding for birding and you might tick green pigeon, Schalow's turaco and a variety of other species.

Accommodation is also available at **Caprivi Cabins River Lodge** and **Hippo Lodge**, both situated on the banks of the Kavango River, a few kilometres east of Katima. **Kalizo Lodge**, about 37km (23 miles) further east along the river, offers fully-inclusive fishing and canoeing safaris.

Impalila Island Lodge

Situated on Impalila Island in the far northeastern corner of Namibia, **Impalila Island Lodge** offers personalized service and a fine wilderness experience. En suite chalets overlook the Zambezi, and activities include tiger fishing, guided walks on the island, mokoro trips, sundowner cruises and viewing the prolific game of Botswana's Chobe National Park from the Chobe River. Birding is outstanding, and species include the slaty egret, rock pratincole, African skimmer, rosy-throated longclaw, greater swamp warbler, Pel's fishing owl, wattled crane, western banded snake eagle as well as the coppery-tailed coucal.

Above: *Tourists negotiate the wetlands in four-wheel-drive vehicles.*
Opposite: *A dugout canoe, or mokoro, on the flood-plain of the Linyanti River.*

BIRDS OF EASTERN CAPRIVI

With habitats ranging from woodlands to floodplain grasslands and riverine forests, more than 440 bird species, including several Okavango Delta 'specials', have been recorded in the eastern Caprivi. The region is a birder's paradise and some examples of the more noteworthy birds that have been recorded here are the slaty egret, coppery-tailed coucal, wattled crane, Pel's fishing owl, copper sunbird, southern brown-throated weaver and red-throated twinspot.

Kavango and Caprivi at a Glance

In **summer** high temperatures and humidity can be unbearable, but are tempered when rain sets in. Exploring off-the-beaten-track destinations is trying in the rainy season as large areas are flooded and tracks are muddy. Bird-watching is most rewarding during summer.
In **winter** the weather is pleasant with cool early morning and evening and pleasant daytime temperatures. The dry winter months are best for game-viewing.

Katima Mulilo is served by regular **Air Namibia** flights, tel: (061) 2996444.
There are **landing strips** near all the major lodges in the area. Other lodges will collect guests at Katima Mulilo airport by prior arrangement.
For **air charter**, contact (in Windhoek) Comav, tel: (061) 227512, fax: 245612; Desert Air, tel: (061) 228101, fax: 248316; and Westair, tel: (061) 221091, fax: 232778. In Swakopmund, contact Pleasure Flights, tel and fax: (064) 404500.

A four-wheel-drive vehicle is essential to explore off-the-beaten-track destinations in the Kavango and Caprivi regions, and it is also essential that you travel in a party of at least two vehicles.
Car hire is available from

Avis, tel: (067) 220520, or from Imperial, tel: (067) 220728 in Tsumeb.
Unless you have quite a large amount of time at your disposal and are very well prepared, probably the best thing to do would be to join an **organized safari** or to stay at one of the lodges in the area, all of which offer guided game-viewing drives, walks and boat trips.
A **tarred road**, approximately 700km (435 miles) long, links Windhoek and Rundu; the 520km (325-mile) **Trans-Caprivi Highway** from Rundu to Katima Mulilo is fully tarred. The route that goes through **Bushmanland** and **Khaudum Game Park** is accessible to four-wheel-drive vehicles only. The Namibia/Botswana **border posts** Mohembo and Ngoma, as well as the Namibia/Zambia border post Wenela, are open every day, 06:00 to 18:00.

Kavango
Sarasungu River Lodge, located 4km (2.5 miles) to the northeast of Rundu on banks of the Kavango River: offers its visitors comfortable reed and thatch bungalows, an à la carte restaurant, bar and a swimming pool. Various activities, including canoeing trips and good birding opportunities are available for guests. Tel: (066) 255161.
Kavango River Lodge, Rundu:

self-catering accommodation with views over the Kavango River, tel and fax: (066) 255244.
Ngandu Safari Lodge, Rundu, overlooking the Kavango River: accommodation ranges from luxury en-suite units to self-catering facilities, tel: (066) 256723, fax: 256726.
Suclabo Okavango Lodge, overlooking the Kavango River near Popa Falls: comfortable chalets, restaurant, bar, viewing deck and swimming pool. Boat trips on river and game viewing to Mahango. tel: (061) 375300, fax: 375333.

Caprivi
Caprivi Cabins River Lodge, 5km (3 miles) from Katima Mulilo: on banks of Zambezi River; offers thatched bungalows with en suite facilities, tel: (066) 252288.
Hippo Lodge, 6km (4 miles) east of Katima Mulilo: on the Zambezi River; has brick-and-reed huts with en-suite facilities, a camp site, an open-air à la carte restaurant, a bar, and a swimming pool, tel and fax: (066) 253684.
Lianshulu Lodge and **Lianshulu Bush Lodge**, Mudumu National Park: overlooks Lianshulu Lagoon on the Kwando River and has rustic reed-and-wood chalets with en-suite facilities; there is also a dining area, lounge and bar, tel: (061) 254317, fax: 254980.
Impalila Island Lodge, on Impalila Island in extreme east of Namibia: on Zambezi

Kavango and Caprivi at a Glance

River; wood chalets with en suite facilities, swimming pool; fishing, birding, boat trips, game-viewing, tel and fax: (27 11) 7067207.

Susuwe Island Lodge, on a small island in the Kwando River: luxury accommodation in thatched chalets with en suite facilities, wooden deck, plunge pool, nature walks, game drives, boat trips, good birding, tel: (27 11) 7067207.

Zambezi Lodge, in Katima Mulilo: offers accommodation on the banks of the Zambezi River in comfortable en suite rooms, also camp sites, restaurant, floating bar, swimming pool, nine-hole golf course, gym and sauna, tel: (066) 253149, fax: 253631.

WHERE TO EAT

Restaurants and various accommodation establishments in Rundu and Katima Mulilo serve meals.

TOURS AND EXCURSIONS

Kalizo Lodge offers fishing on the Zambezi River, boating, birding and trips to Victoria Falls and other destinations, tel: (066) 686802.

Lianshulu Lodge and **Lianshulu Bush Lodge** offer nature drives, walks, night drives, boat trips on the Kwando and bird-watching, tel: (061) 254317.

Impalila Island Lodge offers fishing, excellent birding, walks, boat trips and game-viewing, tel: (27 11) 7067207.

Suclabo Okavango Lodge offers boat trips and fishing on the Kavango River, and game-viewing drives to Mahango Game Park, tel/fax: (061) 375300.

Self-drive tours of Caprivi and the Kavango are organized by Ondese Travel and Safaris, PO Box 6196, Ausspannplatz, Windhoek, tel: (061) 220876, fax: 239700; a **fly-in safari** to Caprivi is offered by Namib Travel Shop, tel: (061) 226174, fax: 239455; Sense of Africa, tel: (061) 275300, also offers a **four-wheel-drive tour** of Caprivi that includes the Chobe National Park in Botswana and the Victoria Falls in Zimbabwe; SWA Safaris, tel: (061) 221193, fax: 225387, operates **safari tours** of Caprivi and Botswana that include a day excursion to the Victoria Falls in Zimbabwe. Before you venture off to explore off-the-beaten-track destinations make sure that you are well equipped and prepared: contact the Surveyor-General, situated on the corner of Robert Mugabe Avenue and Dr AB May Street,

Windhoek, tel: (061) 245056, fax: 249802, for **topographical maps**; the **Automobile Association** (AA), located on the corner of Independence Avenue and Fidel Castro Street, tel: (061) 224201, fax: 222446, provides members with useful travel information; Camping Hire Namibia in Windhoek, tel: (061) 252995, has a wide range of **camping equipment** for hire.

SELECT READING LIST

Birds of the Eastern Caprivi by J. H. Koen.
Bushmen: A Changing Way of Life by Anthony Bannister and David Lewis-Williams.
Popular Checklist of the Birds of South West Africa/Namibia by A. J. Williams.
Sasol Birds of Southern Africa by Ian Sinclair.

USEFUL TELEPHONE NUMBERS

Ministry of Environment and Tourism, Katima Mulilo, tel: (066) 253027.
Namibia Wildlife Resorts, Windhoek, tel: (061) 236975 for reservations and information.

RUNDU	J	F	M	A	M	J	J	A	S	O	N	D
AVERAGE TEMP. °F	77	75	75	73	66	61	61	66	73	79	79	77
AVERAGE TEMP. °C	25	24	24	23	19	16	16	19	23	26	26	25
HOURS OF SUN DAILY	7	7	8	9	10	10	11	10	9	9	8	8
RAINFALL in	6	6	3.5	1.5	0.5	0	0	0	0	1	2	3.5
RAINFALL mm	146	148	87	38	12	0	0	0	2	20	58	85
DAYS OF RAINFALL	16	16	12	6	2	0	0	0	1	5	9	12
HUMIDITY	68	72	69	62	53	50	46	39	33	38	53	61

Travel Tips

Tourist Information

Namibia Tourism has offices in South Africa (Johannesburg and Cape Town), the United Kingdom (London) and Germany (Bad Homburg). The Namibia Tourism Board's office in Windhoek is on the ground floor of the Sanlam Centre, corner of Fidel Castro and Werner List streets, tel: (061) 2906000, fax: 254848. e-mail: info@ namibiatourism.com.na

Regional tourism and publicity associations are represented in a number of towns: **Windhoek Information and Publicity**, tel: (061) 2902092; **Southern Tourist Forum**, tel: (063) 221266; **Lüderitz Information Bureau**, tel: (063) 202532; **Tsumeb Tourism Centre**, tel: (067) 220728; **Namib I** in Swakopmund, tel: (064) 404827 and **Rundu Tourism Centre**, tel: (066) 256140.

Reservations for state-owned accommodation in game parks and resorts are handled by the central reservations office of **Namibia Wildlife Resorts** in Erkrath Building, 189 Independence Avenue, Windhoek. Written applications must be directed to Reservations, Private Bag 13267, Windhoek, tel: (061) 236975. Namibia Wildlife Resorts also has an office in Swakopmund, tel: (064) 402172.

Entry Requirements

All visitors must have a valid passport, and temporary residence permits for visitors are issued on arrival and allow tourists a period of 90 days in the country. Bona fide tourists and business travellers of these countries are exempted from visa requirements: Angola, Australia, Austria, Belgium, Botswana, Brazil, Canada, Cuba, Denmark, France, Germany, Iceland, Ireland, Italy, Japan, Kenya, Lesotho, Lichtenstein, Luxembourg, Malawi, Malaysia, Mozambique, Netherlands, New Zealand, Norway, Portugal, Russia, Singapore, South Africa, Spain, Swaziland, Switzerland, Tanzania, United Kingdom, United States of America, Zambia, Zimbabwe. Visitors are, however, advised to confirm visa requirements with their travel agent.

Health Requirements

Vaccinations against smallpox, cholera and yellow fever are not required. However, visitors travelling from or through countries where yellow fever is endemic must have a valid International Certificate of Vaccination. This requirement does not apply to air travellers in transit. No AIDS screening tests are conducted.

Air Travel

Hosea Kutako International Airport, 45km (28 miles) west of the capital, is the major point of entry into Namibia (*see page 42*). Eros Airport, 4km (2.5 miles) from the city centre, is served by domestic flights. Air Namibia, the national carrier, has regular scheduled flights to Katima Mulilo, Lüderitz, Ondangwa, Oranjemund, and Walvis Bay. There are landing strips throughout the country and air-charter services are available in Windhoek, Swakopmund and Walvis Bay (*see page 42*).

Road Travel

Namibia has a well-developed road system, covering some 40,000km (24,856 miles). Trunk roads covering 5000km (3107 miles) are tarred and connect all the main centres, while major gravel-surface roads are generally in a good condition. The state of district and farm roads varies from good to poor, depending on when they were last graded. Motoring tips: During the summer months care should be exercised on gravel-surface roads as washaways are common after rains. Motorists should look out for wild or domestic animals as they can cause serious accidents. Warthogs feed in the long grass alongside the road and are in the habit of suddenly crossing it. Kudu are a danger at night in densely vegetated areas, and warning signs should be heeded. In rural areas, domestic animals are not fenced so be careful. Always carry emergency spares and sufficient water (at least 10 litres; 2.6 gallons) with you, especially on the lonely back roads.

Driver's licence: The carrying of driver's licences is compulsory. Foreign licences are acceptable if they carry a photograph and are either printed in English or accompanied by an English-language certificate of authenticity. An alternative is to obtain an International Driving Permit before departing for Namibia. Licences issued in Botswana, Lesotho, South Africa, Swaziland and Zimbabwe are valid in Namibia.

Road rules and signs: In Namibia one drives on the left-hand side of the road. Speed limits are 120kph (75mph) on major roads and 60kph (37mph) in urban areas, unless otherwise indicated. Depending on the condition of gravel-surface roads, the recommended speed is between 80kph (50mph) and 100kph (62mph). All proclaimed routes are numbered (major routes with the prefix B, secondary routes with prefix C, district roads with prefix D and farm roads with prefix P or F), and tourist attractions are generally well marked.

Car hire: Avis, Budget Europcar, Hertz and Imperial are represented in Windhoek and have branches in most major towns throughout the country. Several companies specialize in four-wheel-drive vehicles, and Britz: Namibia rents out campervans. Telephone numbers are given in the At a Glance section of each chapter.

Insurance: Third-party insurance is included in the price of fuel. The excess for damage to hired vehicles is high as most driving is on gravel roads with high accident rates. When making reservations, establish the excess and the renter's responsibility in respect of collision damage waiver insurance. Maps: The road map published by the AA of Namibia is useful, and there are several commercially published maps of the country. The *Globetrotter Travel Map of Namibia* is excellent, as is the *MapStudio Touring Atlas of Namibia*.

Petrol: Petrol is available at filling stations throughout Namibia. In Windhoek and some of the larger towns fuel is available 24 hours a day, but in some of the smaller towns and settlements pumps close at 18:00, while restricted hours could apply during weekends. The availability of fuel at some settlements in remote areas is unreliable at times and you should ensure that you have sufficient fuel to get to your destination. In the northwest of Namibia petrol is available only at Ruacana, Sesfontein and Opuwo. Cash only is accepted for petrol in rural areas.

Automobile Association of Namibia: The AAN office is in the Carl List Building, on the corner of Independence Avenue and Fidel Castro Street, tel: (061) 224201. The AA has tow-in service contractors in all major towns. The after-hours breakdown number is: (061) 224201. Maps of Namibia and other southern African countries are also available.

Coach travel: Intercape Mainliner operates a luxury coach service between Windhoek and Walvis Bay, and between Windhoek and Victoria Falls. There are also regular coach departures from the capital to Cape Town and Johannesburg in South Africa.

What to Wear

During the day dress is usually casual, but in some of the more sophisticated hotel restaurants and bars, jeans, T-shirts and slip-slops are not acceptable in the evening when 'smart casual' clothes are the norm.

Early mornings and evenings can be cold during winter (May to September), so pack warm clothing such as trousers, long-sleeved shirts, a jersey or anorak. During the hot summer months (October to April) loose-fitting clothes, a wide-rimmed hat and a raincoat are essential. After rain, temperatures drop by quite a few degrees so include a light jersey for the occasional cool summer evening. Mosquitoes can be troublesome during summer, so remember to pack loose-fitting trousers and long-sleeved shirts to protect legs and arms during the evenings. Warm clothing is necessary throughout the year along the coast where fog and a chilly breeze can create unpleasant conditions.

Money Matters

The Namibian currency unit is the Namibia dollar (N$), divided into 100 cents. Coins are issued in denominations of 5c, 10c, 50c, $1 and $5; notes in denominations of $10, $50 and $100. The Namibia dollar has the same value as the South African rand, which is still legal tender in Namibia.

Currency exchange: Foreign currency can be converted into Namibia dollars at banks and bureaux de change in Windhoek. No foreign currencies are accepted at state-owned rest camps, nor are facilities to exchange foreign currency available. Hosea Kutako International Airport has currency-exchange

facilities. Namibian currency should be converted to foreign currency before leaving the country.

Banks: First National Bank and Standard Bank are represented throughout Namibia. Banking hours are from 09:00 to 15:30 on weekdays and 08:30 to 11:00 on Saturdays, except in country towns where banks close between 13:00 and 14:00.

Travellers' cheques: may be cashed at any bank and at major hotels in Windhoek. State-owned rest camps and resorts will only cash travellers' cheques in South African rand.

Credit cards: Most hotels, restaurants, shops, car-hire firms and tour operators accept international credit cards (American Express, Visa, Diners Club and MasterCard). Some German-owned businesses, guest farms in remote areas and shops in rural areas do not accept credit cards. Petrol cannot be bought with a credit card; some banks, however, issue a special

'Petrocard' or 'Autocard'.

Value Added Tax: VAT of 15 per cent is payable on most goods and services, but visitors may claim VAT refunds.

Tipping: It is customary to tip porters, waiters, waitresses, taxi drivers, room attendants and golf caddies, provided the service is satisfactory. It is usual to tip petrol attendants about N$2 when they offer to clean car windows or to check the water, oil and tyre pressure. Gratuities for waiters/waitresses and taxi drivers are usually 10 per cent of the bill, and tips for porterage are around N$2 per bag.

Accommodation

All accommodation establishments in Namibia, including hotels, pensions (private hotels), guest farms, rest camps and caravan parks, are graded. All accommodation establishments in Namibia must be registered with the Namibia Tourism Board to ensure that high standards are maintained. Provision is made for registration in 13 categories ranging from backpackers hostels, bed-and-

CONVERSION CHART		
FROM	**TO**	**MULTIPLY BY**
Millimetres	Inches	0.0394
Metres	Yards	1.0936
Metres	Feet	3.281
Kilometres	Miles	0.6214
Hectares	Acres	2.471
Litres	Pints	1.760
Kilograms	Pounds	2.205
Tonnes	Tons	0.984
To convert Celsius to Fahrenheit: x 9 ÷ 5 + 32		

breakfasts, guest houses and camp sites to hotels, guest farms and lodges. There is also an increasing number of self-catering facilities.

Hotel pensions must have at least 10, but not more than 20 rooms and must serve breakfast. Accommodation in rest camps is provided in rooms, rondavels, bungalows or other accommodation units and may also include camping sites. Guest farms are known for their typical Namibian hospitality and offer guests an opportunity to experience farm life and to participate in farming activities. Lodges are located in rural areas or within a natural environment and must provide recreational facilities such as game drives, a health spa or other activities. Namib Sun Hotels, Namibia Country Lodges, United Africa Hospitality, Wilderness Safaris and Leading Lodges of Africa have establishments throughout the country. Most lodges, permanent tented camps and tented lodges cater for the luxury market.

Rest camps and resorts: Rest camps and resorts in state-owned conservation areas are run by Namibia Wildlife Resorts, a commercial public company, tel: (061) 236975 for reservations and information. Accommodation ranging from modern bungalows to rustic thatched huts is provided in nearly all state-owned game parks, reserves and resorts, and camp sites with facilities are provided in rest camps, except at Terrace Bay.

Bedding and towels are provided at all the rest camps (except Von Bach Dam Resort and Khaudum Game Park) but no crockery, cutlery or cooking utensils. The major rest camps and resorts all have à la carte restaurants serving breakfast, lunch and dinner.

Public Holidays

New Year's Day (1 January)
Independence Day (21 March)
Good Friday
Easter Monday
Workers' Day (1 May)
Cassinga Day (4 May)
Ascension Day
Africa Day (25 May)
Heroes' Day (26 August)
Human Rights Day (10 December)
Christmas Day (25 December)
Family Day (26 December)

Trading Hours

Normal business hours are from 08:00 or 08:30 to 17:00 or 17:30 Mondays to Fridays and 08:00 to 13:00 on Saturdays. Shops are closed on Sundays and public holidays, but most supermarkets have restricted trading hours on Sundays and public holidays.

Measurements

Namibia, like the rest of southern Africa, uses the metric system.

Telephones

Namibia's country dialling code for overseas callers is 264. The telecommunications

system in the major towns is fully automated and calls can be made to over 200 countries. Dialling inside Namibia is fully automated except to a few remote settlements. Dialling codes, telephone numbers, fax numbers and telex numbers are listed in one directory, available at any post office, for the entire country. Public coin and card phones are available throughout the country.
Enquiries: For numbers that have changed or are not listed in the telephone directory, dial 1188.

Time

In summer, Namibian Standard Time is two hours ahead of Greenwich Mean Time and the same as South African Standard Time; in winter, Namibian Standard Time is one hour ahead of Greenwich Mean Time and thus one hour behind South African Standard Time. Summer time commences at 02:00 on the first Sunday of September; winter time commences at 02:00 on the first Sunday of April.

Electricity

Electrical appliances operate on 220/240 volts. Plugs are 3-pin (round), 15 amp. Not all electric shavers will fit hotel and game-park plug points, and visitors are advised to seek advice from a local electrical supplier.

Medical Services

It is advisable to take out medical insurance before your departure for Namibia.

Hospitals: Windhoek has three private hospitals, the Roman Catholic Hospital in Werner List Street, Medi-Clinic in Erospark and the Rhino Park Private Hospital. There is a Medi-Clinic in Otjiwarongo, and Swakopmund has the Cottage Private Hospital. In Walvis Bay is the Welwitschia Hospital. Tsumeb also has a private hospital. Some churches in the north of the country run hospitals or clinics, and there are state hospitals in major towns. Emergency evacuation is expensive and visitors should ensure that they have adequate insurance, including emergency evacuation.

Doctors: Medical practitioners are listed in the orange pages in the telephone directory.

Pharmacies: All major towns have pharmacies, usually open during normal business hours; some pharmacies in Windhoek have extended trading hours. In rural areas medication is often available only from the state hospital or clinic.

Health Hazards

Malaria: Malaria is endemic in the east, north and north-east of the country and it is important to take precautions throughout the year. The disease is epidemic from the Etosha Pan westwards and in the northern parts of Kaokoland, occurring in particular during the rainy season. As the recommended antimalarial drugs could change from time to time, it is important to consult your doctor or a pharmacist well in advance. It is equally important to take the tablets as prescribed and to continue taking the tablets for the advised period after leaving the malaria area.

Bilharzia: This waterborne parasite attacks the bladder, intestines and other organs of humans, livestock and game. It is found in still water (like dams), stagnant water (like pools) and slow-moving water in some parts of rivers. So, avoid swimming, drinking or washing in dams and rivers.

AIDS: Considering the size of Namibia's population, the number of HIV positive cases is relatively high. However, if the necessary precautions are taken, visitors need not fear contracting the disease. All blood is screened for hepatitis and AIDS by the Blood Transfusion Service of Namibia. The blood is tested by qualified staff according to standard, internationally recognized methods, and is regularly submitted to strict quality controls.

Creepy crawlies: A wide variety of snakes, scorpions, spiders and stinging insects occur in Namibia, but most bites and stings will only cause discomfort. The chances of being bitten or stung are most likely when you are camping out in the open or undertaking walks and trails, and can be minimized by taking a few simple precautions.

Avoid scorpion bites by shaking out your shoes or boots before putting them on in the morning, and do not walk around barefoot or without a torch at night. Ticks are mainly encountered in grassy areas but being bitten does not mean that you will get tick-bite fever. The possibility of tick bites can be reduced by wearing long trousers and by inspecting your clothes and body thoroughly during rest stops and at the end of the day. Remove ticks as soon as possible after they are detected by pulling them away from the body or covering them with a greasy substance.

Emergencies

The national emergency number for the Police is 10111, while the numbers of ambulance services in major towns are listed in the telephone directory on the page preceding subscribers' numbers in the particular town. The two personal crisis help services in Windhoek, Alcoholics Anonymous and Lifeline, are also listed in the telephone directory.

Security

As a rule it is quite safe to walk around the streets of Windhoek and other towns after dark without fear of being attacked, although isolated incidents do occur from time to time so some basic precautions are advisable. Avoid looking like the typical tourist, do not carry large amounts of cash on your person and hand valuables in for safekeeping at hotels. In some rural areas petty thieving has become a problem, so do not leave camping gear and other valuables unattended; rather lock them away.

INDEX

AbaHuab campsite 83
Agate Beach 54
Ai-Ais 5, **50**
Alte Feste 32
Altstadt area 54
Ameib Farm 94
Angolan civil war 15, 17
apartheid 14
armed struggle 12, 15
Aus **49**

Bagani 112
balloon safari **70**
Bethanie **49**
Bird Island **64**
bird-watching 34, **38**, 41,
   65, 102, **113**, 114, 117
black-faced impala 102
black rhino 85, 102
blue wildebeest 102
Bogenfels Arch **57**
Bondelswart Nama 13, 14
Bosau Pass 35
Brandberg 6, 77, **81**
Brukkaros 45, **46**
Bull's Party 94
Burnt Mountain **84**
Bushmanland 109, 110,
   116
Bushman's Paradise 80
Bwabwata National Park
   114

Camel Farm 64
camping tips 67, **111**
canoeing 45, 51, 119
Cão, Diego 12, 79
Carp Cliff 69
Cape Cross Seal Reserve 5,
   79, 82
Cape Frio 87
Caprivi 6, 109, **115**, **116**
Caprivi Art Centre 116,
   119
Caprivi Game Park 115
Cassinga 12, **16**
chestnut-banded plover **66**
Chobe National Park 109,
   118, 119
Chobe River 119
Christuskirche 32
Clay Castles 87
clock tower 31
Constitution 11, 18, 19
cuca shops **105**

Cuito Cuanavale 17
Daan Viljoen Game Park **34**
Damara dik-dik 102
Damara tern 67, 73, 77, 79
Damara Tower 63
Damaraland 5, 77, **80**
desert elephants **85**, 87
Desert to Desert Trail 48
Diamond Coast 52
Dias Point 54
Dinosaur Tracks 93, 95
Dolfynpark **64**
Dorslandboom 111
Dune Seven **66**
Dunedin Star 98
Duwisib Castle **39**

ekipa buttons **26**
elections 18, 19
Elephant Head 94
elephant's trunk 9
Elizabeth Bay 56, **57**
Enyandi rapids 89
Epupa Falls 89, **90**
Equestrian Memorial 32
Erkrath Building 31
Erongo Mountain 93, 94
Erongos **94**
Etendeka Mountain Camp
   85
Etosha National Park 5,
   10, 93, **99**
   accommodation **100**
   vegetation **103**
   waterholes of **104**
   wildlife **101**
Etosha Pan **99**

Farm Dieprivier 73
Felsenkirche 54
Finger Rock **84**
First World War camp 49
Fish River Canyon 8, **50**
Fish River Canyon Back-
   packing Trail 45, **50**
Fish River Canyon
   Conservation Area 52
fishing **7**, **21**, 78, 88, **117**
forced removals 12, 14
Franke Tower 94

game-viewing **34**, 38, 40,
   85, 95, 96, 111, 115, 117
   and safety 99, **114**
Gamsberg mountain 6
Gamsberg Pass 35
Gathemann House 31
gemsbok **10**

Geneva Protocol 18
Giant's Playground **47**
Gibeon meteorites 31
Goerke House 53
Gondana Cañon Park 49
Grootboom 111
Grootfontein 93, 97
Grootfontein museum 97
Gross Barmen 29, **41**
Gross Barmen Mission
   Station **41**
guano islands **58**

Halali 100, 103
Hardap Dam and Recrea-
   tion Resort 8, 29, **37**
Hardap Game Reserve 38
Hartmann Valley 89
Heinitzburg 33
Henties Bay 8, 78
Herero 12, 13, 23, **25**, 30,
   40, **94**
Himba 23, **25**, **89**
Hippo Lodge 119
Hoanib River 86
Hoba Meteorite 8, 93, **97**
Hobas 50
Hobatere Game Park 86
Hobatere Lodge 86
Hofmeyer Walk 30
Hohenzollernhaus 62
Holboom 104, 111
Hollam's Bird Island 79
horse trails **35**, 52
Hotel Kronprinz 31

Impalila Island 119
Independence Avenue 30
International Court of
   Justice 12, **15**
Intu Afrika Game Lodge 37

jetty (Swakopmund) 63
Johanitter Haus 48
Jonker Afrikaner Nama 30
Joseph Fredericks House 49

Kalahari 6, 45
Kalahari Gemsbok
   National Park 37
Kalizo Safari Camp 119
Kaokoland 5, 77, **89**
Kapuuo, Clemens **40**
karakul sheep **48**
Katima Mulilo 109, **118**
Katutura 14, **31**
Kavango 109, **111**
Kavango River 7, 113–115

Kavango woodcarvers 40
Keetmanshoop 45, **48**
Khaudum Game Park 5, 10,
   109, **111**
Khoikhoi 12
Khomas Hochland 6, 29, **35**
Khorixas **82**
Khowarib Schlucht **86**
Kolmanskop **55**
Kongola 116
Königstein 6, 8, 82
Kreplin House 54
Kuiseb Canyon **69**
Kunene River 7, 89
Kutako, Hosea **40**
Kwando River 7, 115, 117,
   118

Lake Guinas 98
Lake Oponono 105
Lake Otjikoto 93, 98
Langstrand **64**
Lianshulu Lodge 117
lichen fields 67, 73, 77,
   79, 82
Liebig Haus 35
lighthouse (Dias Point) 54
lighthouse (Swakopmund)
   62
Linyanti Swamps 7, 118
lions **101**
Lizauli Traditional Village
   116, 117
Lüderitz 5, 7, 8, 12, 20,
   45, **53**
   water supply for **55**
Lüderitz Museum 54
Lüderitz Peninsula 54
Lüderitzbucht Foundation
   56
Lutheran Church (Keet-
   manshoop) 48

Mahango Game Reserve
   5, 109, 113
Maltahöhe **39**
Mamili National Park 112,
   116, **118**
Mandate 12, 13
Mandume, Chief 14
Marienfluss 89
Mariental 37
Martin Luther 62
Mata Mata 37
Mbanderu Processions 29,
   40, 94
Mbanguru Woodcarvers'
   Co-operative 112, 116

Mile Four 78
mining 8, **98**, **56**
Mokuti Lodge 103
Molkte-Blick 6
Moon Landscape 68
moringa tree **103**
Morrell, Benjamin **58**
Mount Etjo Declaration 18
Mount Etjo Safari Lodge 95
mountain zebra **71**
Möwe Bay 20
Mudumu National Park **117**
Mukurob **46**
Multi-Party Conference 16

Namaland 46
Namib Desert 5, 45, 61
  animals of 71, **73**
  conservation of **67**, **79**
Namib Dune Sea **71**
Namib Publicity and
  Tourism Association 63
Namib-Naukluft Park 10,
  61, **66**
Namibia Crafts Centre 33
NamibRand Nature
  Reserve 73
Namushasha Lodge **116**
Namutoni **100**, 103
!nara **9**, 26
National Art Gallery of
  Namibia 33
National Theatre of
  Namibia 33
National West Coast
  Recreation Area 77, **78**
Naukluft Mountains 5, 61,
  70
Ndonga people 13
Noordoewer 51

Odendaal Plan **14**
Okahandja 29, **41**
Okaukuejo 100, 103
Okonjima 95
Old Post Office 49
old school building 32
Old Station Building
  (Lüderitz) 54
Oanob Dam 36
Ohangwena 105
Omaruru 93, **94**
Ombudsman's Office 32
Omeg Minenburö 97
Omusati 105
Ondangwa 105
Ondorusu rapids 89
Ongava Lodge 102, 104

Ongongo Falls **86**
Ongwediva 105
Ontouka Reptile Park 104
Oorlam Nama 12
OPO 14
Opuwo 90
Orange River 7, 45, **51**
Oranjemund 8, 53, 56
Organ Pipes **84**
Oshakati 105
Oshana 105
Oshikoto 105
Otavi Mountains 93
Otjihaenamaperero Farm
  95
Otjihipa mountain 89
Otjikoto tilapia 98
Otjiwarongo 96
Owambo 93, **105**
Owambo people 24
Owela Museum Display
  Centre 32

padrão 12, 79
Pager, Harald 82
Palm Beach 63
Palmwag Lodge **85**
per capita income 19
Petrified Forest **82**
Phillip's Cave 94
plateau, the 6
Popa Falls 7, 109,
  113, 114
population density 23
Post Street Mall 31
puku 112
Purros 89

quiver tree 9, **47**
Quiver Tree Forests **47**

recreation **26**
red lechwe 112
Reho Spa **36**
Rehoboth 29, **36**
Rehoboth Museum 37
religion **23**
Resolution 435, 12, 16–18
Resolution 2145, 12
Rhenish Mission Church
  Bethanie 49
  Omaruru 95
Rhenish Mission House 95
Richtersveld National Park
  52
roaring dunes 87
rock art 12, 77, **80**, **83**, 93
rock lobster 21, **54**

Rössing Mine 64
Ruacana Falls 8, 89, **90**
Rundu 112, 116

salt works 64, 65
San 12, 23, **24**, 109, 110,
  115
sand dunes **72**
Sanderburg 33
sandroses 55
Sandwich Harbour 5, 7,
  61, **67**
Schmelen House 49
Schutzenhaus 49
Schwerinsburg 33
Second Director's House 97
Second World War 14
Sesfontein **86**
Sesriem Canyon 5, 61, **72**
Shark Island 54
Sheltering Desert **69**
shipwrecks 87, **88**
shopping
  Caprivi **116**
  Lüderitz **53**
  Swakopmund **63**
  Windhoek **33**
sitatunga 112
Skeleton Coast 77
Skeleton Coast Park 5, **87**
social services **22**
Sossusvlei 5, 8, 61, **72**
Southern Tourist Forum 49
Space Theatre 33
Sperrgebiet 52, 56
Spitzkoppe **80**
sport **26**
Spreetshoogte pass 36
St Barbara's Catholic
  Church 97
Stampriet 37
State House 62
State Museum **32**
stone plants 9
Suclabo Lodge **113**, 114
Susuwe Island Lodge 115
Swakopmund 5, 8, 61, **62**
Swakopmund Museum 63
Swakopmund railway
  station 62
SWANU 14
SWAPO 15

Terrace Bay 87
Tintenpalast 32
Tjokwe 110
Topnaars **25**
Torra Bay 87

Trans-Caprivi Highway 20
Transitional Government
  of National Unity 12, 16
Trans-Kalahari Highway 20
transport **19**
Trilateral Agreement 17, 18
Tsauchab River 72
Tsumasa Hill 103
Tsumeb 93, 97
Tsumeb Museum 98
Tsumkwe 110
Turnhalle Conference 16
Twyfelfontein 77, **83**

UN Council for South
  West Africa 15
UNTAG **17**, 18
urbanization 19
Us Pass 35
Uugongo Art Centre 53

vegetation **9**
Victoria Falls 7, 109, **118**,
  119
Von François Fort 35
Von Trotha extermination
  order 12, **13**

walking trails 34, 47, 66,
  70, 81, 82, 83, 88, **96**,
  104
Walvis Bay 7, 8, 12, 18,
  20, 61, **65**
Walvis Bay Wetlands **65**
Warehouse Theatre 33
Warmquelle **86**
Waterberg Plateau Park
  93, **96**
waterbuck 112
Weissrand plateau 46
welwitschia 9, **68**, 82, 83
Welwitschia Drive 68
White Elephant frieze 94
White Lady Procession **81**
wild horses **52**
wildlife **10**
Windhoek 5, 29, **30**
Windhoek Information
  and Publicity (WIP) 31
Witbooi, Hendrik 13
Wlotkas Baken 78
Woermannhaus 62, 63

Zambezi Lodge 119
Zambezi Queen **119**
Zambezi River 7, 118, 119
Zebra mountains 89
Zoo Park 30, 31